peaceful spaces

alice whately

peaceful spaces

transform your home into a haven of calm and tranquillity

RYLAND
PETERS
& SMALL

LONDON NEW YORK

For Barty, with all my love

First published in the United Kingdom in 2002
by Ryland Peters & Small
20–21 Jockey's Fields
London WC1R 4BW
This compact edition published 2005
www.rylandpeters.com

10 9 8 7 6 5 4 3 2 1
Design, text and photographs
© Ryland Peters & Small 2002, 2005

ISBN 1 84172 991 4

A CIP record for this book is available from the
British Library

Printed and bound in China

Picture credits
Front Jacket: photographer David
Montgomery/Belinda and Guy Battle's house,
designed by Mathew Priestman

For this edition:

Senior designer Sally Powell

Senior editor Clare Double

Picture research Tracy Ogino

Production Sheila Smith

Art director Gabriella Le Grazie

Publishing director Alison Starling

CONTENTS

Since ancient times, the home has provided a sense of belonging, affection and togetherness around which we are able to structure our lives. Today, this concept is more important than ever as the frenetic pace of modern living increases our desire to retreat to a soothing haven where we can nurture mind, body and soul.

introduction

As a result, the creation of a peaceful environment is at the forefront of contemporary design requirements. Taking its inspiration from the dictates of Zen minimalism, this soothing style combines spontaneous simplicity with natural materials in order to create an effective antidote to the stresses and strains of life in the twenty-first century.

Otherworldly though it may sound, there is no great mystery to the creation of the 'soul home'. Instead, it is a simple case of paring down your interior in order to allow the intrinsic beauty of light, texture and shape to form the decoration. Neither is the concept of a spiritual environment confined to the bedroom or living area. Instead, this design directive is a holistic one – as applicable in the home office as it is in the bathroom – enabling you to create the sort of serene retreat you thought was the exclusive domain of the luxury health spa.

the theory

'Space and light and order. These are the things men need just as much as they need bread or a place to sleep.'

LE CORBUSIER (1887–1965)

space clearing

By questioning the purpose of everything you own, you will quickly realize that it is you, rather than the stuff that surrounds you, that must take centre stage in the home.

Commonly viewed as a Japanese concept, Zen philosophy actually originated in China, where monks merged Indian Buddhism and Chinese Taoism in a bid to find the true path to spiritual enlightenment. In 1190, Zen Buddhism was enthusiastically adopted by the Japanese, who developed the idea that simplicity was synonymous with spirituality and applied it to every aspect of their lives – including their homes.

The sense of harmony found in Zen's design style transmits similar feelings of serenity to its occupants – and has been reinterpreted by Western designers and architects since the nineteenth century. Today, the Zen interior has become a refuge from the outside world where busy roads, new technology and the cult of consumerism leaves us feeling anxious and unfulfilled.

As a result, more and more of us are turning to the ancient philosophies of the Far East in order to regain a sense of spirituality in our domestic lives. Increasingly, our homes are becoming places of sanctuary where simple Zen aesthetics help to calm the senses, inspire creativity and induce clarity of thought.

CREATING A BLANK CANVAS

In order to turn your home into a haven of peace and tranquillity, you must first look closely at the availability of space and light. To do this, walk slowly through each room; scrutinize the floors, walls and windows, and consider the following options. Are there any walls you could knock through or replace with loadbearing pillars? Is it possible to insert more windows or to raise the height of existing ones? Could you install a skylight? Does your carpet cover space-enhancing boards or antique parquet?

Next, look at your furniture, fixtures and fittings and ask yourself what you could do without. If you're scrupulously honest, you may well discover that many things you thought were indispensable to domestic bliss are, in fact, easily made redundant.

The theory of space clearing combines the physical process of removing unnecessary clutter with the aesthetic one of simplifying your surroundings. For example, if you use the same colour for your walls and floors, your home will immediately feel calmer and more cohesive. Similarly, if you employ flexible devices, such as sliding doors, pull-out shelves, fold-up tables and wheeled units, your space will instantly appear sleeker and more streamlined.

It is also important to think laterally. Necessary 'white goods' don't have to fit into their allocated rooms just because tradition demands it. For example, if you have a tiny kitchen, plumb your washing machine into a bathroom cupboard, or keep your tumble

A single colour scheme in a living area (opposite) enables the jutting angles of the fireplace, sloping roof and timbered ceiling to combine seamlessly for a coherent whole. A white-on-white room also makes your space look bigger, allowing for the addition of a large sofa, comfortable chairs and a smattering of gently curved objects, which soften the look.

Again, white effectively opens up a space, giving a narrow corridor through the kitchen (above) a feeling of lightness and expansiveness. The overall look is much more workaday than the floaty feel of the living room next door, thanks to the scrubbed wooden table and worktop. In addition, darkly coloured ornaments help anchor the look.

dryer in a cupboard under the stairs if you're pushed for space elsewhere.

When it comes to making decisions about your home, it's important to listen to your instincts. This way you will reconnect with your spiritual self – and create an environment that nurtures your heart and soul. By stripping your home of the things that fail to inspire you, you make space for the things that do. If you love books, for instance, celebrate your literary leanings by building a huge bookcase. Similarly, if music soothes your soul, install a huge sofa and allow yourself to listen in comfort and peace.

CLUTTER CRUSHES THE SPIRIT

The philosophy of clearing your space and hence your mind is one that works for most people. According to Zen principles, clutter is an accumulation of anything that impedes the vital flow of 'chi' – or essential energy – in the

What could be a dingy staircase is actually an attractive feature (above)**, thanks to the combination of pale scrubbed wood and white-painted walls. The knots and gnarls in the wood add extra interest, as do the colourful native masks sitting on the landing shelf.**

The elegant lines of an art-school plan chest (right) **provide excellent storage space. Here, the calming symmetry of the slim drawers is balanced by a handful of natural ornaments – an unframed canvas, an air-purifying orchid, woodcarvings and fossil fragments – to produce a look that is as calm as it is aesthetic.**

Not only do the floaty drapes offer a feeling of softness to the minimalist bedroom (opposite)**, but they also help to diffuse harsh light, creating an ambience of tranquillity.**

The heavy appearance of a dark wooden tallboy (far left) is given a fresh and contemporary feel through the addition of a brace of wicker baskets. The soft curves of the chair and light tones of the natural floor covering also help to lift the look.

A skylight (left) is an ideal way to ensure that your space is filled with natural light. The flood of sunlight also provides a connection to the natural world which, together with the introduction of greenery, is essential for attaining a feeling of spiritual vitality within the home.

home. Without the presence of chi, it is impossible to turn your living environment into a place where your thoughts and actions are spirited and spontaneous.

In order to attain a clutter-free space, you must first prune your possessions with the religious zeal of one determined to see the light. Anything you no longer use, want or like should either be thrown away or taken to the charity shop. This includes shoes, clothes and kitchenware, as well as CDs you no longer listen to, photographs that will never make it into the album, and books you're unlikely to read. It is also important to rid your home of negative energy, which is manifested through plants that are dead or dying and anything that has been broken for a long time or has parts missing.

17

THE POWER OF WHITE

Think of any peaceful space designed to nurture the spirit – be it a yoga studio, a chapel, a spiritual retreat or a holistic spa – and you can be sure its walls will be painted a light, bright shade of white. The colour of purity, cleanliness and peace, white is key to creating a spiritual environment, offering a sense of luminosity that acts as an effective salve for the soul.

The advantages of living in a serene white cube are numerous. Not only do walls painted in pale shades reflect natural light, making your space seem bigger and brighter, but continuity of colour also

continuity of colour prevents fragmentation

prevents fragmentation. Avoid the bluish tint of ultra-white, however, as it can seem cold and stark unless you live in a sunny country. Instead, opt for creamier tones, which will help turn your home into a sanctuary of softness and warmth.

An all-white colour scheme also allows for a multitude of textural contrasts. For example, juxtapose untreated concrete walls with a shiny lacquered floor to create a shell of subtle contradictions, or pair a white wicker chair with a pristine silk cushion for a look that is interestingly discreet rather than bland and boring. Sticking to a pale palette also allows for the creation of instantly dramatic focal points through the occasional bolt of brilliant colour. For instance, contrast a vase of orange gerberas or a jewel-bright rug against a blank canvas and – hey presto – your decoration is complete.

A white and cream colour scheme (above) **illustrates the strong impact of pared-down decoration. The flimsy cotton blind allows for lots of natural illumination, while a pebble and the antiquated jug, filled with a simple bunch of daisies, create a focal point.**

Textural contrast is vital in the all-white room (right)**, where the roughly painted wood table and bumpy wicker chairs are juxtaposed with the sheer fabric of the curtains and smooth surface of the milk bottle, beakers and shiny plates.**

Clearing clutter in the
workspace is essential for
creating an atmosphere that is
conducive to concentration
(this page). Here, a selection of
box files, plus a couple of sets
of small filing drawers, keep
things in their place without
appearing overly regimented.
The desktop is kept clear, save
for vital pieces of equipment.

A selection of attractive spiral-bound notebooks and a pretty floral paperweight (left) help to keep your thoughts – and paperwork – in order, and prove that organization in the peaceful workspace does not need to look dull and 'officey' to be effective.

Not only are box files (below) a great way for filing office paperwork, but they can also be used for storing magazines. In this orderly office, a combination of labelled box files and lidded storage boxes is ranged along neat cubicle shelving, providing the user with quick and easy access to important documents and periodicals. The soft aqua colour range is a calming departure from the more masculine colours often associated with office storage.

SALVATION THROUGH STORAGE

However diligently you clear your clutter, you will still need storage space for functional items such as linen, blankets, DIY tools, cleaning products, stationery and paperwork, which all need to be stowed away. It is also important to remember that you will need more storage than you think. Collections of books, CDs, ceramics and shoes never get smaller, only larger, and situations change (you may want to start a family, a new hobby, a fitness regime – all of which require additional space).

The good news about modern storage is its spiritually sympathetic design. Buy a built-in cupboard these days, and you get a beautifully streamlined piece of furniture that adds to, rather than detracts from, the cohesive look you want to achieve. Better still, most modern units come with pop-open door mechanisms or flush-fit handles, enabling your cupboards to blend seamlessly with the room's overall decor.

Another option is to implement structural storage that fits into the framework of your space. This can be achieved by replacing partition walls with floor-to-ceiling units accessible from both sides. Modular compartments provide a mix of open and shut storage space, while recessed shelving gives a truly streamlined result.

Once you start exploring the potential for storage in your home, you will discover an abundance of 'dead areas' begging to be exploited. For example, slot drawers or a large chest beneath the bed; install a pull-out

Structural storage that fits into the framework of your space (opposite) **is a wonderful way to keep clutter hidden from view, while wall-to-wall storage units are ideal for streamlining your space. In addition, fold-away or multi-functional furniture will help to keep your living areas as clear as possible.**

Modern-day units need not be dull simply because they are functional; instead, make a feature of your storage solutions by choosing contemporary cubes (below) **and stacking them in a seemingly spontaneous tower, supported by a central rod. In this way you will achieve excellent storage that is also attractive.**

Natural light is an essential feature in the creation of a peaceful living environment (right and opposite), helping to generate energy, amplify space and nurture the soul. In addition, according to the philosophy of feng shui, a daily dose of fresh air is essential for ridding your home of stale yin energy. As a result, it is imperative that you harness as much light as possible, and it is worth considering installing more windows or increasing the size of existing ones in your home. Alternatively, you can also explore the possibilities of French windows, skylights or a conservatory.

laundry bin under the bathroom basin; or sidestep the need for a dressing table by creating a niche – complete with electric points – in a bedroom cupboard.

HEAVENLY CONTAINERS

The calming home has a cohesive appearance. It should be a place where your eyes and mind can roam free from the constraints of consumerism. To attain this purity of vision, it is essential that you keep vulgar packaging to a minimum (nothing jars like the lurid logo of a domestic cleaner). Decant everything you buy into attractive containers and your home will become an instantly – and blissfully – brand-free zone.

It doesn't matter what containers you choose to decant into, as long as you group similar ones together. For example, transfer dry goods such as pasta, flour, rice and cereal into identical glass jars; put washing-up liquid, cotton-wool balls and toothpaste into sisal or wicker pots, and fill ceramic bottles – complete with dispensing pumps – with shampoo, conditioner, moisturizer and liquid soap.

SEEING THE LIGHT

Consider any soulful experience – biblical or otherwise – and you will find that it has a strong dependence on the purity of light. As a result, it is easy to see why light is a key factor in the creation of a home that will nurture the spirit: light helps to harness energy, to amplify space and to generate feelings of optimism and goodwill.

The best illumination for your space and for your spirit is daylight, a natural phenomenon that should be exploited to the full. This means exploring the possibilities of installing more windows, increasing the size of existing ones and introducing skylights. Alternatively, take the light-enhancing process a step further and construct a conservatory.

It is also possible to maximize daylight by keeping windows as clean and clear as possible: if you have curtains, tie them back during the day or, better still, replace them with light-filtering blinds. In addition, keep the exterior of your windows clear by pruning vines and creepers. Move light-blocking pieces of furniture to the other side of the room and ensure that your windowsills are kept free of ornaments.

If you are unable to keep your windows completely clear – you may be overlooked by

The beneficial impact of colour on our mood is well documented by psychologists around the world. Combine colour with light, however, and the effect on the psyche is truly remarkable. A bedroom painted blue (this page) **creates a serene sense of peace** and tranquillity, while the pretty diamond patterns created by the honeycomb glass ceiling (opposite) **are not only aesthetically attractive but also help to promote feelings of optimism and energy, thanks to the shifting nature of the warm patches of light.**

neighbours, for example – cover the bottom half of the windows with a semi-opaque fabric, such as linen, cotton or muslin. Similarly, if the glare is too harsh, try Venetian blinds, sandblasted glass or tracing paper – all of which help diffuse light and create thought-provoking shadows.

In terms of artificial lighting, a strictly minimalist approach is advised: replace overhead lights with subtle uplighters; choose wall-mounted lights over table lamps to keep surfaces clear; and wire lights to circuits operated from a single panel in order to reduce the need for ugly sockets and trailing flexes. You can further extend the range of your lighting by fitting bulbs of varying wattage, controlled by individual circuits.

MOOD HUES

The concept of matching your lighting to your mood is a seductive one. Better still, thanks to hip hoteliers Ian Schrager and Philippe Starck it is now a realistic option in the home. Kicking off with the Mondrian in Los Angeles, where coloured light installations funk up the hotel's clean white space, the design duo have taken the concept a step further at London hostelry, St Martin's Lane, which allows guests to illuminate their clinical white rooms by dialling up the colour of their choice.

Even better, Colorwash, the lighting system used by Schrager and Starck, is now available in the shops – enabling homeowners to mood-light their interiors in subtle tones that can be changed from blue to violet and red to green at the flick of a switch.

Slim vertical wires provide a calming complement to the angles of the staircase (below), while the round bowl and disc-shaped holes carved into the wooden plinths also provide a soothing contrast in this basically neutral space. To add further interest, woods have been chosen in varying grains and hues.

By carefully choosing and positioning your furnishings, you will discover the beauty in harmony and simplicity.

balance and form

To achieve harmony in the home, it is vital to create a balance between form and function. This concept derives from the Zen aesthetic of yin and yang or, in layman's terms, opposing forces which, when equally represented, create a harmonious balance of energy.

The energy in our homes is in a constant state of flux, so achieving the perfect balance between yin (cool, dark and lifeless) and yang (hot, bright and full of life) is essential if we are to create a calming and cosmic atmosphere. The best way to introduce both yin and yang into the home is through the natural elements of fire, water, earth, metal and wood – the fundamental types of energy found in all substances and phenomena. When these elements are equally represented, their synergy will create the vitally spiritual environment we seek.

It is not necessary to introduce the five elements into your home in their raw states, however. Instead, each can be represented symbolically, using colour or texture. For

The sinuous curves of a plain ceramic vase (top) cast a wonderful two-toned shadow, while the uncompromising lines of the lamp (above) are softened by the burnt-umber shade.

The forces of yin and yang are represented (right) through the use of colour: the orange discs in the paintings signify fire; and the brown background, earth. Similarly, the turquoise cushion represents water, and the spray of blossom symbolizes wood.

example, if you don't have enough space for an indoor water feature, use an indigo cushion or a turquoise vase in its place. Similarly, fire can be represented by a candle or an orange lantern; earth, by pebbles; wood, by house plants; and metal, by a silver photo frame.

Spiritual energy is also wrought through the force of contradiction. The collision of new and old, hot and cold, and decorative and plain, all create an electrical current that runs between opposites. A good example of this is the energy charge created by the use of contrasting colours. This works particularly well with a predominantly neutral palette, where the juxtaposition of pink and yellow or brown and turquoise gives potentially bland spaces a life-enhancing jolt.

In a perfect example of balance and form, the decorative objects surrounding the fireplace (this page) work on a number of different levels. The serene symmetry of the lacquered jars provides a smooth complement to the coarser fibres of the shallow basket placed in the grate, and their glossy sheen is echoed in the black frame of the picture propped up against the wall. Rigid lines contrast with soft curves to compound the effect, while the jars' off-centre positioning creates a balanced whole.

A sure way to enhance energy in the home is to use contrasting colours (opposite). Here, the combination of sea blue with yellow kick-starts an otherwise sombre room, effectively preventing the dark woods from dominating.

According to the philosophy of feng shui, large mirrors are an excellent way to generate positive yang energy in a living area (far left). Not only do they make your space appear larger and lighter, but their reflection also adds an extra dimension of interest.

To create a naturally balanced living environment, it is necessary that the five elements of wood, water, fire, earth and metal be represented (left). Here, the timber table, candles, stone holders and mats, cutlery and water glasses fit the bill perfectly.

In order to negate the harsh rigidity of the modern world, where technological equipment dominates, it is important that you balance hard lines with soft curves to create a more conducive environment in your home (above).

A potentially harsh monochrome colour theme (below) is softened thanks to a collection of natural objects that have been arranged on the shelf above the fireplace. The vertical arrangement of driftwood balances the horizontal cluster of shells, while the circle pattern on the cushion softens the look further.

It is perfectly possible to use pattern (right) without making your space look overly busy. Here, the large floor cushions – made from vintage kimonos – provide an ideal complement to the bouffant spray of blossom arranged in an elegant vase.

DECORATING WITH A SIXTH SENSE

Feng shui has been practised for the past four thousand years and derives from the Chinese Taoist science of divining the healthy and prosperous layout of the home. This means decorating in order to harness 'chi' (the vital life force) and avoid 'sha' (noxious vapours).

If the energy in your home becomes blocked – or allowed to flow too swiftly – it can cause corresponding blockages and problems in life. Luckily, misspent energy is easily corrected. At its core, feng shui teaches that, by making small shifts to the arrangement of furniture and decorative accessories in your home, it is possible to improve your relationships, spiritual development, health and finances.

An uncluttered bedroom is essential for getting the best out of your downtime (below). **Here, the simple furnishings are prevented from appearing bland thanks to an inspired palette, which contrasts pink, yellow and grey-blue to create an ultimately restful effect. In addition, the pastel-coloured picture makes a powerful statement without appearing too forceful.**

decorate your space for health, harmony and happiness

Although it is extremely fashionable to employ the services of a feng shui expert, it is also possible to correct the flow of energy in your home without the aid of a professional. Not only are there numerous books on the subject, but the basic principles are reasonably straightforward – and will go a long way towards the creation of a spontaneously vital environment. Use the following pointers to balance energy in the home.

• Avoid putting your bed under a window; this will disrupt the energies around you and make your sleep disturbed.
• Arrange sofas and chairs to form a square, as L-shaped layouts are inauspicious.
• Large mirrors are excellent for enhancing energy in a small space. However, do not place a mirror on a wall that reflects the door, as this will dissipate energy.
• Balance straight lines with curves to soften the technological blow of the modern world.

35

The different sizes and shapes of the alcoves carved into the wall (far right) provide the perfect framework for a collection of exquisite ceramics. In addition, their colours create pleasing contrasts of light and shade against the white wall.

Images of a similar style – be they prints, photographs or postcards – look great clustered together (above). Make sure that each is simply framed – and remember that arty images do not need to be hanging on a wall to create a striking effect; overlapping postcards, propped up on a windowsill, can be just as arresting. The rough texture of the pebbles provides a calming complement to the clean, smooth finish of the frames, while their organic shapes and varying sizes contrast with the rigid style and identical proportions of the three images.

• Place quartz crystals (considered the aspirins of feng shui) on sharp edges, such as the corner of a desk, to dissipate bad chi.

• Open two windows in two different rooms at least twice a week. This way you will enable fresh yang air to sweep away stale yin air.

• While fresh flowers bring yang energy into living spaces, they can also become depressingly yin once they wither. Replace fading flowers with fresh ones as soon as they start to lose their vitality.

THE ART OF OBJECT ARRANGEMENT

The creative arrangement of objects is an excellent way of achieving harmonious yin and yang energy in your home. Better still, a small collection of everyday items, such as flowers, fruit or shells, is preferable to expensive shop-bought ones as their impact is wrought by their intrinsic beauty, rather than through a contrived and artificial display. Votive candles, shells and pebbles look their best when clustered together. Choose soft colours and pure shapes that relate well to one another and to the space around them – a jade Buddha next to a white plate, for example. Displaying similar objects in varying degrees of size is effective – a collection of three baskets in large, medium and small, for instance; or use this approach for displaying vases, glasses, bowls and framed prints.

Displaying objects within the framework of an alcove or fireplace is another aesthetic choice, while contrasting textures and forms – a rough piece of driftwood with a smooth pebble, or a cashmere throw across the back of an upright chair – make for perennially attractive combinations.

Balance is also important, although layout does not have to be regimented. Even numbers create a calming symmetry, while odd numbers add interest. Varying the colour and height of objects also works well: juxtapose strong, dark colours with lighter, more translucent ones,

Natural objects, such as shells, pebbles and seed pods, are preferable to man-made pieces, thanks to their ability to evoke memories of walks along a sandy beach or time spent in a sunlit garden. Contrasting rough textures with smooth ones is a tried-and-tested formula in the creation of a pleasing space, and is beautifully illustrated by two shells set together (left) – one showing its shiny interior expanse, the other its grainier exterior. Similarly, the glass jars and lacquered dish (below) soften the coarser surface of the timber table, while the rough pumice stones (below left) contrast with a work surface that has been finished in smooth ceramic tiles.

Autumn leaves laid across a coarsely woven runner (above) make a simple table decoration. The intrinsic beauty of found objects cannot be imitated by artificial means.

A simple rustic-style glass-fronted cabinet (right) makes an ideal display case for a collection of objects in earthy shades. Pleasing contrasts in height, texture and shape combine to create an ultimately sophisticated result.

or place a couple of tall vases with a few mid-height jars to create an interesting perspective.

When it comes to picture-hanging, a more rigid approach is required. If you have a good-sized wall, hang one large picture dead centre and leave it at that. Alternatively, a set of prints by the same artist looks great hanging in a group, as long as each is similarly framed. If you choose to hang pictures by different artists, try to keep within the same family of colours, and allow them to breathe by giving each image adequate wall space.

A CORNER FOR CONTEMPLATION
In tandem with the ever-increasing pace of the world comes a desire to find fundamental meaning in our lives through the ritual of contemplation. As a result, personal shrines are becoming a popular way for homeowners to find peace and reconnect with their spiritual selves.

shrines need to evolve with your spiritual growth

The secret of creating a shrine is to find a quiet place where you can meditate for at least fifteen minutes a day. If your home is large enough, set aside one room in which to meditate. If not, furnish a quiet corner with a floor cushion and table on which to display significant objects. These should include representations of the five elements. Ideas include: a feather to symbolize the uplifting effect of air; a filled vase or bowl to symbolize the cleansing properties of water; a candle to symbolize the transforming aspect of fire; sand, salt or stones to symbolize the grounding qualities of earth; and a coin or silver photo frame to symbolize the neutralizing properties of metal.

Your eyes and heart will tell you when you have selected the right balance of objects. Over time you may find that some of your treasures appear to lose their vitality

Your area of contemplation (above) should contain up to a dozen of your favourite objects, and may include a figurine or image of a deity. The five elements – earth, water, fire, metal and wood – should also be represented, in order to create a calming balance of yin and yang. It is advisable to include a flower or plant, as this will encourage spiritual growth and help you to connect with the natural world.

Even the most mundane corner of your home (opposite) **can take on a shrine-like quality of calm through the thoughtful selection and placement of ornaments.**

and need to be replaced. This is because
shrines represent your spiritual growth and
so must evolve as you do. For example, the
treasured collection of shells you picked up on
a beach in Bali may become less important if
you take another holiday to an equally magical
place. Similarly, a token given to you by a
loved one will lose its effect if your relationship
cools off. As a result, it's important to spend
time tending your shrine and making it reflect
you, since this mirrors your attitude towards
your spiritual development.

THE DIVINE IS IN THE DETAIL
Thanks to their intrinsically beautiful qualities
of form and colour, the most inspiring objects
often derive from the world of nature. The
bloom of a peach or the beauty of a tightly
furled bud are a source of wonder even
though their appearance may be imperfect.
In addition, these details are often rich in
personal association – a feather found on
holiday or a pebble picked up from a
windswept beach both have a significance
that goes far beyond material value.

The meticulous decor of the tranquil living
space is perfect for sharpening our powers of
observation, allowing us to perceive the
beauty in everyday objects that might be
overlooked in a more cluttered environment.
For example, a collection of shells simply
displayed in a glass dish can evoke the
mystical energy of the moon and sea, as
does a silvery piece of flotsam that has been
weathered by time and tide. Similarly, old
wooden furniture that has been polished to

It is not necessary to create an elaborate display in order to reap the beneficial effects of flowers – a single stem placed in a glass tumbler (above left) **will enhance your living space just as effectively.**

A pared-down decor allows us to appreciate the beauty of a few treasured objects (below left). **Here, the polished sheen of an antique chest highlights the grain of the** wood, while the impact of the decorative egg-shaped ornament is enhanced by the elegantly spare lines of the modern lamp beside it.

An almost perfectly symmetrical display (below) **formed of two framed photographs and a pair of oak plinths is cleverly completed and complemented by the contrasting shapes of the two substantial beeswax candles.**

a high sheen enables us to appreciate its texture, grain and flaws, as well as giving us a reassuring sense of stability and comfort through its age-old associations with nobility, wisdom and strength. By the same token, hand-thrown ceramics, carvings hewn from grainy wood and lovingly embroidered rugs all have a similar intuitive appeal. Because we know they have been created by hand with care and attention, we appreciate the irregularities that give each piece its own uniqueness and identity.

appreciate the beauty in natural details and found objects

Flowers are a beautiful and inspiring way to introduce natural details into the home. Not only are they exquisite to look at, but they also encourage spiritual awakening and generate energy. The most effective include: chrysanthemum to help concentrate the mind; lotus to open channels of spiritual consciousness; iris to promote spiritual integration; rose for love; black-eyed Susan to awaken spiritual consciousness; angels' trumpets to promote spiritual initiation; and angelica for guidance from divine realms.

Polished stones or gemstones have been used on altars for thousands of years in the belief that each releases a unique energy. Stones that exude particular spiritual powers include: emeralds for healing; lapis lazuli for intuition; bloodstone for strength; quartz crystals for attunement; and rubies for strength, health and spiritual passion.

Contrast the waxy texture of candles with rough stone holders and glassy pebbles, and opt for scented varieties as the use of fragrance enhances peaceful feelings. Aromatherapy also comes in the form of incense sticks, which offer a simple way to imbue your living space with spiritual feelings as well as adding a hint of exotica.

ETERNAL FLAMES

For thousands of years, candles were an essential part of everyday life – illuminating dark nights and representing faith and hope in religious rituals across the world. Today, candlelight is an important feature in the home, representing the divine spark within us and helping to ignite our imaginations through the magical evocation of shadows.

There are numerous types of candle available on the market. Good options for use in meditation or the creation of a tranquil and calming atmosphere include coloured flowers that float in water, sculptural blocks with four or five wicks apiece and elegant beeswax tapers, which promote a church-like feel when pushed into a bowl of sand. Similarly, small tealights in coloured glass containers give an incandescent glow, while a cluster of votive candles creates a galaxy of seemingly divine illuminations.

DIVINE FRAGRANCE

Known to boost our sense of well-being, the use of fragrance can help us to turn our homes into havens of sensory perception, creating an uplifting environment when we need to be stimulated, and a calming one when relaxation is called for. Better still, the choice of olfactory products on offer is guaranteed to lift the spirits, providing sweet-smelling aromas in the form of vaporizers, candles, pot pourri, herb-filled pillows, joss sticks and incense cones.

Scented candles are the most popular way to fragrance your space; you can even opt for the feng shui variety, with the essences of fire, water, metal, earth and air. Aromatherapy candles scented with jasmine, orange blossom, frangipani, honeysuckle and lily of the valley are also effective mood-enhancers, while spicy-smelling candles imbue the atmosphere with amber, musk and cinnamon.

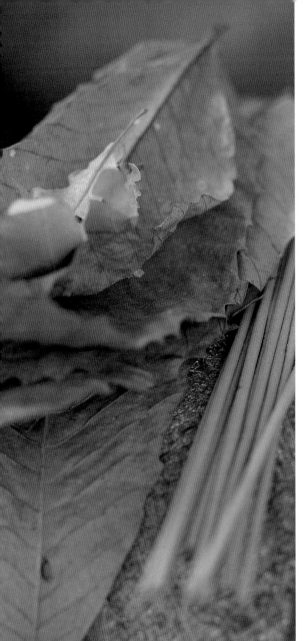

Floating candles shaped like flower heads and combined with petals and blooms are an attractive and effective way to introduce the Zen elements of water and fire into your home (left and below). Reminiscent of age-old meditative practices in the Far East, candlelight helps to promote feelings of spiritual attunement.

use different aromas to encourage feelings of optimism and goodwill, to create a stimulating or a soothing environment

Essential oils are another favourable way to scent your home, thanks to their efficacy at clearing unwanted vibrations. Most potent when they come into contact with heat, vaporizers such as oil burners, electric diffusers or ceramic lightbulb rings emit the fragrance of essential oils consistently and gently. To create an ultimately soulful ambience, try sandalwood for spiritual attunement, frankincense for spiritual clarity and cedar wood for clearing spiritual energies. To soothe the senses, choose geranium, neroli, rose, jasmine, ylang ylang, lavender or camomile.

For thousands of years humans have burned herbs, scented wood resins and other aromatic substances in order to connect with the spirit world through the meditative practice of watching smoke spiral heavenwards. Popular in the hippy-trippy 1960s and 1970s, the fashion for joss sticks is back in vogue, thanks to a renewed desire for spiritual attunement. These days, however, burning incense is a more sophisticated affair: sleek lacquered boxes replace the plastic packets of yesteryear, while scents such as lemongrass and ginger replace the staple aromas of the past – jasmine and patchouli.

Sleekly packaged beeswax candles (left) will burn to fill the room with a subtle but distinctive aroma.

An arrangement of nightlights neatly fitted inside a selection of colourful Moroccan tea glasses (above) will give your living space an incandescent glow, helping to ignite the imagination and generate spiritual energy.

As the fashion for candlelight continues to gather pace, so too does the choice of wax illuminations on offer. Whether you choose to light your home with elegant beeswax tapers or sculptural blocks with five or six wicks apiece (below), candlelight helps to infuse the atmosphere with calming or uplifting aromas as well as to create evocative shadows.

Space, light and natural materials have been used to full effect (left) in order to create the ultimate in spiritual chic. The power of contrast is also exploited, with the smooth concrete of the curvilinear passage juxtaposed against an untreated timber wall and the rigid lines of the windows.

A variety of natural materials has been used to create a restful corner (right), that is both comfortable and aesthetically pleasing.

natural connection

The interaction of organic textures and colours in the home creates an environment that is as spontaneous as it is serene.

Furnishing your home with natural elements is a Zen tradition that is successfully applied in any home seeking to provide sanctuary from the outside world. Materials such as wood, stone, linen and hemp allow us to energize our spaces through the fecundity of the earth and to revel in their rich textures and colours. According to the dictates of Zen living, natural materials stimulate the senses in a way that synthetic ones cannot. Compare, for example, the merits of a cold lino floor with a warm wooden style, and the more attractive option is easy to spot. Similarly, a smooth glass door handle is much more tactile than a tacky plastic one.

By the same token, these criteria for spiritual living are also in tune with the current fashion for eco-chic – a furnishing style which is environmentally friendly and concentrates on the use of organic

Texture and pattern are needed in the peaceful home in order to prevent the space from appearing spartan or bland. Splashes of red, mixed with soft furnishings upholstered in bold checks, gives the log cabin (opposite) an injection of energy, while the smooth lines of the sofa (right) contrast with textured flooring and a patterned throw to give a calming sense of balance. Similarly, the reflective sheen of the polished terracotta tiles (below) provides a cool complement to the warmer appearance of the natural-fibre matting with jute edging.

materials to create a truly soulful space. Homes that are lacking in natural elements will cause their owners to become spiritually deprived – increasing their sense of isolation from the great outdoors.

As far as furniture design is concerned, organic curves are preferable to straight ones, simply because they help us to escape from the rigidity of modern technology where hard lines and sharp corners predominate. That said, if you do choose to take a hard line with your furniture, it is possible to temper the look of straight-up-and-down sofas, chairs and footstools through the use of soft furnishings. Sumptuous upholstery, squashy cushions and casually draped throws – preferably with fringing around the edges – will all reduce the hard appearance of strictly linear furniture. Similarly, the introduction of pattern will also help to divert attention away from sharp edges; choose bold checks, faded florals or sassy stripes for a look that is spontaneous and informal. The canny use of colour is another effective deflector: natural shades such as mulberry, tan and terracotta create the illusion of a calming and coherent whole, while more vibrant colours such as red, purple, turquoise, pink and yellow create arresting focal points.

Far from appearing cold and unyielding, the dark flags of the stone flooring (this page) have been softened thanks to the bold expanse of orange paint on the wall. A slightly brighter variation on traditional terracotta, this colour also helps to lift the pedestrian design of the wooden table and draws attention to the plant pots on the windowsill.

COLOUR YOURSELF CALM

The colours of nature are a prime inspiration in the spiritual home. In order to create a calming ambience, combine base shades with earth ones before seasoning with a splash of sea-blue or a flick of forest green.

Base colours include subtle shades of white erring towards cream, beige, straw, ochre and sand; these can be combined with soft pastels such as pale blues or washes of green for an ultimately soothing effect. Where contrast is required, earth colours, drawn from rocks and soils, are applied. These shades are muted and subtle, varying from the cool whites, greys and pinks of marble, slate and granite, through the yellow tones of desert sands to the warmer rusts and deep reds of monumental rocks.

SPIRITUAL SHADES

Brown Brown creates feelings of solidity and protection through its association with the colour of earth – pigments such as 'sienna', 'umber' and 'ochre' are literally made from the earth. Use it in a newly decorated room to create a warm, lived-in feel. Brown should be used sparingly, however, as too much can cause feelings of depression.

Beige and oatmeal These neutral colours sit well with organic materials such as wood, cane, wicker and stone. Effective stress-busters, beige and oatmeal are both easy to live with. In addition, these pale neutrals reflect light, making your space feel bigger and brighter.

In order to create a sense of coherence, it is important to ensure that transitional spaces such as passages, landings and stairs continue the serene theme. The mystical shade of the blue paint on the stairwell (above right) is an excellent example and illustrates how a simple wash of colour can promote spiritual feelings of lightness and transcendence.

The muted hues of glazed bottles (below right) summon up soft shades of nature, evoking images of green meadows, calm seas and heather-filled moors.

Instead of man-made materials, choose natural ones, such as a feather fan (left), in order to give your home a sense of real soul.

A cool green hall (below) is perfect for creating a smooth link between the upstairs living area and the downstairs one. Known for its perfect balance of yin and yang, green is the ideal colour for transitional areas within the home.

The warm earthy palette in a light-filled bedroom (opposite) creates a naturally restful mood as well as helping to make it appear more spacious. In addition, a neutral colour scheme provides the perfect backdrop for the natural wood furnishings and the Native American artwork.

choose a palette of natural, earthy tones from creamy white to sand, injecting accents of soft blues, greens or reds into a neutral backdrop

Terracotta This rich earth colour is warm and intense and has been a staple furnishing shade for hundreds of years. As a result, terracotta has a timeless feel and creates an air of primitive vibrancy without being overbearing.

Blue Arguably the most spiritual colour of the spectrum, blue triggers the release of eleven tranquillizing hormones in the body. It is also linked to the spirituality of the moon, together with white, silver and indigo.

Green Green symbolizes regeneration and spiritual growth. As well as being restful on the eyes, it contains equal proportions of yin and yang, helping to balance energy and promote harmony.

Violet Violet calms the spirit at its deepest level. It also helps to soothe the body and mind and is often used in meditation rooms.

Yellow Yellow buoys the spirit and engenders feelings of optimism. It is also one of the most effective ways to brighten a room that is deprived of natural light.

The cohesive and pristine appearance of pale wooden boards, timber window frames and a long wooden table (opposite) is saved from blandness thanks to the reflective sheen of the polished floor and the uneven edge of the table.

Offering the perfect corner for contemplation, the ultimate organic seat (above right) was carved from an old tree trunk and fits into its curvy setting with reassuring solidity.

Knotted and whorled with age, the timber planks that make up the log cabin (left) offer enough interest and variation to sustain wall-to-ceiling coverage.

The walnut-faced bentwood arms that wrap the classic butterfly-shaped chair (above) in a graceful embrace also provide a smooth contrast to the darker, more deeply ingrained seat and back, and prevent the design from appearing too spindly.

TREE OF LIFE

Throughout history, trees have been viewed as the axis through which divine energy flows from the supernatural world to the natural one. As a result, it's hardly surprising that wood is a key element in a spiritual space, helping to promote feelings of stability and comfort through its age-old associations with nobility and strength. When it is young and green, wood exudes energy and growth. As it gets older and more seasoned, it becomes imbued with wisdom and spirituality, lending credence to the ancient belief that each tree has its own soul. Better still, there are numerous varieties of timber on the market, each offering its own brand of colour, scent, texture and grain. Different woods summon different atmospheres. For example, if you want to create a calming feel, opt for pale light-reflecting timbers such as bleached driftwood or golden pine.

Offering a funky alternative to conventional stone flags, pebbles embedded in a concrete bathroom floor (below) **conjure up breezy beach walks. Conversely, the bamboo panel evokes a Far Eastern feel. The unusual combination puts a fresh spin on bringing the outside indoors.**

A blue-and-cream-striped flatweave cotton runner (left) **gives the grey floorboards of a peacefully bare bathroom a new lease of life.**

Timber boards present an endlessly streamlined flooring option and provide the perfect base for contrasting different textures such as this abaca rug (below) **overlaid with woven wool that has been felted and shrunk.**

A white concrete floor with a single stripe detail of cobbles provides the ideal base for a minimalist bedroom with an exotic feel (opposite)**.**

A homely ambience is best achieved with richly coloured woods that add warmth and security, while dark woods such as time-worn oak or gleaming ebony promote safe feelings of intimacy and seclusion.

GETTING GROUNDED

Thanks to their calming linearity, timber boards are a great way to spiritualize your space. Better still, they can be employed in a variety of ways to create different looks. Use them on your floors, walls and ceilings to create the intimacy of a cosy log cabin, or limewash dark boards to open out small interiors and create a feeling of lightness and expansion. The continuous appearance of stripped boards also works brilliantly with wooden furniture carved from a different grain or hue, providing a textural contrast that is spontaneous and natural.

stone is imbued with feelings of strength, solidity and stability

Mixing and matching different types of stone is a great way to showcase the variations available. The combination of hard slate with soft sandstone (opposite)**, together with a couple of sea-moulded rocks, creates a soothing symphony of colour, shape and texture.**

If you can afford stone flagging (below)**, choose the largest pavers you can find, in order to create a feeling of smooth serenity.**

If wooden boards are not a possibility for flooring, try laying compressed bamboo instead. Not only is this wood strong and durable, but it is also water-resistant and aesthetically pleasing. Alternative 'green' flooring includes cork, which is waterproof as well as inexpensive and naturally sustainable, and woollen felt, which is hardwearing and offers excellent sound insulation.

The vogue for natural materials has prompted a revival of one of the oldest forms of flooring known to man – rush matting. Also available in jute, sisal, coir and seagrass, these fibrous coverings work well thanks to their organic texture, earthy colours and adherence to the Zen dictate of combining form with function.

ROCK OF AGES

Given its seeming immutability, it's not surprising that stone is linked to the building of sacred structures such as temples, shrines and cathedrals. By the same token, its qualities of permanence and tradition make it a quintessential feature in modern interiors.

The popular image of stone – cool, pale and smooth – is belied by its wonderful variety of colours, textures and patterns. Capable of appearing fresh and inviting or warm and earthy, stone helps to 'ground' your home in a number of ways, depending on the state of your finances. For example, the spiritual homeowner with a healthy bank balance should consider laying flagged paving in his or her hall, living area or bathroom, while less expensive options include installing marble

Complete with a
wonderfully fine linear
grain, the silky-smooth
organic curves of a
sinuous chaise longue
in teak wood (this page)
are further emphasized
by its more solid branch-
like supports.

Contrasting a variety of natural textures is a simple way to create a haven of sensory pleasure with seemingly little effort. A shorn sheepskin floor rug complements the unfinished edges of the roughly hewn wood lounger (below).

The distressed appearance of an old painted wooden dining table, combined with thick, fibrous placemats and the gently curving edges of a smooth stone bowl (right), creates a soft and calming display – a perfect setting for relaxed dining.

counters in the kitchen, a limestone sink in the bathroom or terrazzo tiles in the toilet. Even a terracotta urn or a vase filled with pebbles will help to imbue your space with the mysticism of age-old rock.

NATURAL FABRICS TO SOOTHE THE SENSES
Resilient and attractive, the texture and drape of natural fabrics is almost impossible to imitate by artificial means. Linen, cotton and wool can be woven or knitted into many different looks – from rough and rugged to gossamer-fine and floaty. This versatility brings the textiles of our homes into harmony with nature, helping to suggest warmth in winter and coolness in summer.

In addition, most natural fabrics are able to withstand years of use, often becoming more

Cushions in different colours, patterns and textures (above left) are an effective way to jazz up and bring comfort to a pared-down space. Here, the heathery hues of the woven wool and herringbone tweed introduce a rustic look.

Juxtaposing similar textures can be equally effective. On a natural-fibre flooring, similarly upholstered stool seats (below left) compound the organic look.

attractive with age. Old linen sheets that have softened over time feel much nicer than starchy new ones, while the soft patina of a faded silk quilt invokes the atmosphere of a bygone era. Integrity and quality are key when it comes to choosing furnishing fabrics for the home: opt for the softest cashmere, the finest cotton and the supplest suede to please the senses.

TOUCHY-FEELY TEXTURE AND CONTRAST

One of the best ways to achieve contrast is by following the law of opposites – a method that works especially well if the rooms in your home revolve around a single colour.

Hard and soft

Polished pebbles in a sisal container

A wrought-iron daybed with a fleece-covered mattress

A glass container planted with a feathery fern

Rough and smooth

Coir matting with suede floor cushions

An untreated wooden shelf supporting a row of glass jars

A wicker laundry basket in a marble bathroom

Warm and cool

Leather upholstery on a metal chair

A sheepskin rug on a stone floor

A bright print in a stainless-steel frame

Straight and curved

A streamlined hall with a spiral staircase

A rectangular vase filled with twisted willow

A square table with a round lamp

With its complementary mix
of horizontal and vertical
lines, the decor of the room
(this page) achieves a
pleasingly balanced whole
without appearing contrived.
The streamlined appearance
of the wooden flooring is
echoed in the horizontal
lines of the chair's leather
upholstery, while various
shallow bowls decorate the
top shelves of the alcove.
This is balanced by a
collection of tall vases on
the shelves below, and a
chunky tribal necklace that
has been draped over the
top of the door.

Luxurious and rigorous
A raw-silk cushion on a stone seat
A sinuous vase on a concrete plinth
A mohair throw on a straight-backed sofa
Patterned and plain
Waffle-weave towels in a glass shower cubicle
Exposed brick walls with lacquered shelves
A bouclé sofa with nubuck cushions

LIFE-AFFIRMING FLOWERS

In the future, trend predictors believe that
urban dwellers with no access to a garden will
devote a room to live greenery in a bid to
reconnect with nature. Whether the idea of a
'green room' actually catches on is irrelevant
in the spiritual home, as the inclusion of
plants and flowers is a fundamental feature
that cannot be overlooked. One of the reasons
for this is the Zen belief that plants introduce
the element of wood, which signifies growth
and development, and helps to promote
spiritual well-being.

Flowers are also the most beautiful and
subtle way to scent the home. Fill your space
with sweet-smelling roses, narcissi, freesias
and hyacinths, or plant fragrant shrubs, such
as jasmine or honeysuckle, close to your

window so the scent washes through. Herbs are also wonderfully aromatic: bergamot, lavender, mint, rosemary, sage and thyme give off the nicest smells and can be grown in windowboxes or indoor urns.

The medicinal properties of plants are well documented: use the herbs in your garden to make up your own simple tonics, such as herbal teas, for example. Leafy plants also benefit your environment by purifying the air – drawing in carbon dioxide and replenishing it with oxygen, as well as releasing moisture to prevent your space becoming too dry. In addition, it has been proved that certain house plants can filter the environmental toxins produced by computers and printers, as well as those pollutants caused by cigarette smoke and chemical cleaners. The best purifying plants to include in your space are gerberas, moth orchids, tulips, cyclamens, chrysanthemums, peace lilies, areca palms, spider plants, bamboo palms and rubber plants.

Whether you're a rose fanatic, a herb grower or an ardent horticulturalist, flowers and greenery are vital in the peaceful home, fulfilling a number of criteria to help enhance the feel-good factor of your living environment. Not only are flowers beautiful to look at, but their scent is the subtlest way to fragrance the air. The presence of living greenery also promotes energy and optimism, while leafy plants are one of the most effective ways to purify the atmosphere, drawing in carbon dioxide and replacing it with oxygen.

'Beauty springs from thought and sensibility,
rather than from material wealth.'

CLAUDIO SILVERSTRIN (1954–)

PART TWO

the space

The unique layout of the living space (right) combines weathered wood with faded bricks and earthy tones to create a homely feel, despite the proportions of the room. In addition, the generous array of cushions transforms the cool slate steps into an area for total relaxation, while the low-level coffee table adds a laidback loungey feel.

living

It is important to create a living space that is conducive to good relations: calm and uncluttered on the one hand, comfortable and inviting on the other.

This is the main room of the home, and for this reason your living area is likely to be a hub of social activity – a place where family and friends gather together to exchange news, gossip and ideas. The alternative facet of your living space is its function as a 'quiet room'. This is, after all, the home's premier chill-out zone – a place where you can listen to music, talk on the phone, watch films or simply cogitate on your life.

The primary function of the decor you choose for your living space, like other rooms in the home, is to convey a sense of serenity. The best way to achieve this is to surround yourself with colours and textures that please and calm you. In addition, choose shapes that are easy to live with and try to maintain a harmonious balance between form and function, as this room – by its very nature – is likely to be busier than others in the home.

KICK BACK AND RELAX

In order to maximize the spiritual potential of the living room, aim to create an airy ambience in which to kick back and relax. One of the best ways to promote a spacious look is through the use of natural flooring. Whether you choose coir matting or stone flags, an

The exotica of heavy Far Eastern furnishings sit calmly and comfortably alongside traditional European ones thanks to the symmetrical and formal arrangement of this room. The red-and-cream colour scheme, which is repeated throughout the space, compounds the sense of order, while the different sizes of the pots on the cabinets (below) play a quirky trick on our sense of perspective.

organic base will go a long way towards making your home appear more grounded. As far as the spiritual space is concerned, wood planks are ideal, providing a linear look which is both calming and cohesive. If you're not lucky enough to have floorboards in your home, consider investing in reclaimed planks or in the less expensive option of laminate woodstrip, as a timber base beneath your feet is one of the most effective ways to create a spiritual feel.

Although wooden flooring can feel like a ubiquitous feature in modern interiors, the variety of choice – in terms of colour, texture, grain and finish – means that wood is easily adapted to create a number of different looks. For example, stripped and polished boards give a rustic ambience; whitewashed boards produce an airy romantic feel; dark-stained boards make your space seem safe and intimate; while polished parquet or beech-strip flooring is clean and contemporary.

73

a big sofa is a key feature of the living space, especially if your home's style is pared down with minimal soft furnishings

Although the peaceful space errs towards minimalism, it is a far cry from the spartan principles of Zen living. Instead, fabrics are sybaritic in the extreme (this page), and cosy cashmere throws combine with other natural materials for textural contrast.

Maximize the peaceful potential of your living space by using colours and textures that mesh harmoniously together (opposite). A neutral palette in warm shades; soft furnishings that strike an easy balance between form and function; and ornaments to provide soothingly aesthetic focal points will all create an ultimately conducive ambience for relaxation.

LAYOUTS FOR CLEAN LIVING

It is likely that there will be more furniture in your living space than elsewhere in the home, so it is important to consider the relationship between the individual pieces carefully. The proportions of the room, of course, will need to be taken into account – a vast loft apartment, for example, can accommodate several large pieces of furniture without the overall effect appearing too cluttered. However, a harmony of shape, colour and texture must also be established. This can be simply achieved by balancing hard lines with soft curves, pale shades with brighter ones and smooth surfaces with rough finishes. In this way, you will create an aesthetic balance of yin and yang which, in turn, allows a free flow of cosmic energy throughout your space.

Although they are complementary colours, red and green used together as the dominant colours in a room could jar the senses. However, soft pink against a jade-green sofa (above) makes a restful and welcoming combination.

Despite their scale, the streamlined style of the sofas and chairs in this loft apartment (opposite) creates a feeling of lightness and space, and this is compounded by the navy-and-white colour scheme.

A favourite comfy armchair upholstered in a luxurious fabric, such as raspberry-coloured velvet (left), will maximize the comfort-zone effect. Add a tumbler of soft blooms (above) to complete your sensory enjoyment.

warm honey colours usher in feelings of comfort and hospitality

KEEP COLOURS NEUTRAL

The key to creating a spiritual colour scheme is to find a colour or group of colours with which you feel at peace, and then to work with them as a base. Any pale shade – as long as it is clear and tonal – will provide a soothing backdrop, although for the living area neutrals are often the first choice.

As long as your chairs and tables are of a similar hue, it is possible to mix and match furnishing styles while retaining a cohesive feel. In addition, a neutral palette allows for the addition of almost any other colour, and contrasts particularly well with white, cream, violet and every shade of blue – from indigo to turquoise and aquamarine to duck-egg.

The warm whites and honey tones of the living space (opposite) allow for an eclectic mix of designs that combine to make a peaceful whole. The traditional shutters contrast with the 1960s bubble TV and 1950s steel-and-rope chair, while the spartan layout is softened by the addition of a sumptuous sheepskin throw.

Opting for a basically neutral palette allows for the addition of almost any other colour. The lemon yellow of the gently curved sofa (this page) is a perfect example, compounding the sunny feel of a bright and uplifting living space.

79

SOFTLY, SOFTLY FURNISHINGS

Your living-room sofa will be one of the most used pieces of furniture in your home. So, because you will be spending so much time lounging around on it, finding the right one requires thorough and persistent research. Once you find a style you like, remember to sit on it for at least five minutes in order to test its quality. If you can feel the springs or the frame poking through, then discount it immediately and move on to a different make. It is also important that you check potential seating for adequate spinal support – a squishy sofa may feel great for sinking into when you kick off your shoes after a hard day's graft, but a style that is too soft is likely to cause postural problems in the long term.

The presence of comfortable sofas and chairs in your living space also provides the ideal opportunity to create a restrained feeling of decadence through the addition of luxurious details. For example, upholster your sofa in

Whether you're looking for a huge squashy sofa, a sumptuously spacious armchair or an elegant lounger (above), finding the perfect seating for your living space demands time and effort in order to find a style that looks good, but compromises nothing in comfort.

A simply elegant sofa plus a collection of generous-sized rattan chairs enable the occupants of this pristine living space (right) to lounge or entertain in comfort.

Although the styles of the chair and sofa are different (far left), the patterned upholstery in varying green checks creates a calming link.

Adding a simple bunch of lavender or lilac (left) from the garden will provide a soothing focal point, as well as filling the room with wonderful aromas.

opting for an uncontrived palette allows for the display of different furnishing styles and for the introduction of pattern and discreet touches of luxury

plush velvet to promote a laidback feel, or scatter a daybed with cushions covered in super-soft cashmere for irresistible comfort. Soft furnishings also provide an ideal opportunity to inject a jolt of pattern and colour into your design scheme. Upholstery in cheerful checks is particularly effective, providing warmth and vibrancy within the calming confines of a regimented pattern. By sticking to one range of colours or type of pattern, soft furnishing can also be used to unify different styles of seating within the living area and to counter the potentially cluttered effect of grouping furniture together.

LIVING LIGHT OF THE HEARTH

A fire flickering in the hearth is one of the most effective ways to enhance the atmosphere of your home – as well as providing warmth and offering a soothing and meditative focal point. A log fire is also fabulously aromatic. Not only is the distinctive smell of burning wood calming and therapeutic, but its natural fragrance can be enhanced in a number of ways. For example, add a handful of pine cones or a bunch of dried herbs for a refreshing top-note,

You don't have to stick to a pale palette to create a peaceful look. Faded strong colours are just as effective (above), and enable a mix of patterns to coexist without appearing overdone.

The curving back of the wicker sofa (opposite) is complemented by the rigid lines of the panelling. The arrangement is softened by the distressed surfaces of the faded armoire and sea-green table.

An essentially cool space, with white panelling and bare brickwork, the living area (left) is brought to life by the flickering flames of the fire, which soften the decor and infuse it with an inviting glow.

Logs stored haphazardly beside the fireplace (opposite) add a relaxed rustic feel, in contrast to the grandeur of the antique mirror and delicate stencil work. Bunches of lavender and rosemary are on hand to be thrown into the flames for instant aromatherapy.

the presence of merry, darting flames will imbue your minimalist space with warmth, light and energy

or rub woody essential oils into your logs before burning them, in order to fragrance your space with the scent of cedar wood, cypress, sandalwood or rosewood.

If your living room does not have a working fireplace, or you live in a city where log fires are prohibited, you might want to consider the installation of a gas version. These fires may not give out any real heat, but their lifelike appearance is extremely effective.

Even when your fireplace is not in use – during the summer, for instance – it can still be employed to create a focal point within the room. Simply replace the presence of flickering flames with a still-life display of natural objects: vases of flowers, chunky candles or a collection of wicker baskets all look great when framed within the parameters of the fireplace, and add an earthy organic feel that compounds the elemental look.

Continuing the fiery theme, the slate shelf (below) is dotted with a collection of candles in varying shapes and sizes. Not only does this enhance the monochrome design, but it also adds a number of alternative focal points.

Simple wooden knobs combine with rough paintwork (right) for understated interest.

Chunky pottery, scrubbed wood, freestanding furniture and wicker baskets filled with fruit create a tranquil feel in a rustic-style kitchen (opposite). Compound the look with terracotta paint and limewashed floorboards, and use wooden plate racks for crockery to instil a calming sense of order.

eating

Dining simply in the company of family and friends is one of the fastest routes to relaxation, helping to combat stress and raise the spirits.

The impact of food on our spiritual health is manifest in a number of different ways. A nutritious diet enables us to function at optimum efficiency, while the process of converting raw ingredients into tasty aromatic dishes feeds our creative impulses.

There are no hard-and-fast rules regarding the design of the peaceful eating space. That said, the current fashion for a combined cooking and eating area works particularly well in the soul home simply because it provides a feast for the senses: delicious aromas and visual delights whet the appetite, while an open-plan layout provides a homogenized feel, which helps mind, body and soul to stay connected.

As long as your cooking and eating space remains warm and clutter-free, it is possible to create a feeling of well-being through the creation of two very different styles. If you're the efficient type, the

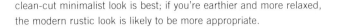

clean-cut minimalist look is best; if you're earthier and more relaxed, the modern rustic look is likely to be more appropriate.

RUSTIC STYLE

The rustic eating space ushers in feelings of warmth and welcome, and home-cooked meals. Freestanding pieces of furniture are favoured over made-to-measure fitted units, while limed floorboards and terracotta tiles replace cool, hard surfaces such as marble and steel.

That said, the modern rustic look is also pared down, relying on a few thoughtfully chosen pieces to evoke a spontaneous shabby-chic look. A warm-toned wooden table provides a reassuring focal point in the earthy kitchen, while an Aga, a butler's sink and a Victorian pine dresser decorated with plates promote a time-honoured feel. The idea is to celebrate the intrinsic beauty of antiquated furnishings in order to imbue your cooking and eating area with an authentic and intuitive feel.

Although the peaceful kitchen is pared down, it also allows for features such as open shelving (far left), where the restful shapes of gleaming stainless-steel canisters and pure white bowls enhance, rather than detract from, the overall effect of calm and efficiency.

The super-sleek eating space of the converted loft (centre) is softened by a calming palette of soft blues and dove grey. In addition, the pale wooden floor and elegant Eames chairs balance out the harsh concrete ceiling, creating a cohesive look that is efficient without being cold.

Opting for a mixed palette of bright colours does not necessarily create a jarring effect. Instead, the structured linearity of the built-in cupboards (left) complements the bold blocks of yellow, pink and green.

In tune with the relaxed style of the rustic cooking and eating space, colour choices are wonderfully wide-ranging. For example, earthy shades of terracotta, sand, buff, beige and biscuit will help to compound the organic look, while sky blues and forest greens are fresh and upbeat. It is also possible to introduce pattern without impinging on the scrubbed wholesome feel. Contrast duck-egg-blue walls with a spriggy tablecloth, for example, or surround an old pine table with simple wood chairs upholstered in bright and cheerful gingham.

WARM AND INTIMATE DETAILS

The rustic cooking/eating space also benefits from a smattering of wholesome accessories. To complete the natural country look, include the following: fresh linen tea towels; wild flowers displayed in a simple clear-glass vase; woven baskets for storing potatoes and apples; old-fashioned storage jars, battered tin tea caddies, French enamel bread and flour bins; chunky peasant pottery; the occasional spriggy print; and old-fashioned creamware.

A great example of Zen style, the cooking and eating area (above) **combines industrial elements with natural ones to create a balanced whole. In addition, the floor-to-ceiling windows ensure that the space is washed with lots of natural light, while the curve of the worktop softens the minimalist look and prevents the space from appearing too spartan.**

Simple glass storage jars (opposite, left) **filled with basic items such as teabags and dried goods add a workaday feel to the streamlined aesthetic of minimalist eating areas.**

Combine plain crockery in soft hues (opposite, right) **with a pair of wooden chopsticks and a linen tablecloth for a naturally aesthetic look.**

ZEN STYLE

If the minimalist look is more your style, then your cooking and eating space should adhere to the Zen aesthetic of combining form with function to create an effective culinary environment. As a result, hi-tech elements combine with natural ones to produce a spiritually soothing interior where drawers roll smoothly on their runners, the gas lights first time, and the knives are always sharp.

It goes without saying that the Zen cooking–eating area is perfectly pared down. In direct contrast to the rustic look, sleek units and acres of clean shiny surfaces create a streamlined effect, while all the unattractive but necessary white goods (the washing machine, fridge and dishwasher) are artfully disguised behind a facade of calming panels. Surface treatments combine the harder

91

Whether you choose ceramics in nature-inspired shades or opt for simple styles lacking in adornment (above), chunky, handmade pottery works brilliantly in the rustic- and Zen-style eating space, compounding the no-frills look in a single move.

by sticking to simple shapes and a neutral palette, it is possible to juxtapose natural elements with contemporary designs finishes of steel, chrome, marble and granite with softer wood tones in warm light hues – beech, maple and cherry wood are all ideal.

By the same token, colours in the Zen cooking–eating space are also chosen for their ability to counteract the sharp efficient edges of contemporary kitchen design. Opt for a palette of one or two shades, and choose calming creams, soothing blues and peaceful shades of green to create a serene effect. In addition, natural floor surfaces – stone, granite and wood – should be kept rug-free, and pattern restricted to occasional decorative ceramics.

PURE AND SIMPLE DETAILS

Although it is an essentially minimalist space, the Zen cooking and eating area does not lack soul. Rather, its stark decor provides a pristine arena where the addition of simple culinary items adds a grounding workaday feel. For a spontaneous Zen look, include the following: airtight Kilner jars for storing dried beans, nuts and pulses; built-in cabinets with attached plate racks for calming linear storage; pure white ceramicware; sparkling uncut glass; simple round doorknobs, either painted or left plain; unadorned chairs; wooden bowls filled with shiny apples; and traditional silver-plated cutlery.

PEACEFUL PLACE SETTINGS

In keeping with the simplicity of spiritual style, your dining area should feature a plain but elegant table as its focal point. Choose a design carved from wood or stone, and ensure that your chairs are made from the same

Contemporary lines and organic elements sit comfortably together within a neutral colour scheme (above)**. For example, the vertical panels of the timber units are echoed in the modern artwork on the walls, while the soft circles of** the earthenware crockery **are picked up by the graphic pattern woven into the rug.**

The worn appearance of the metal canisters (opposite, right) **adds a time-honoured feel to a rustic-style kitchen.**

material or have some link in their design to give a sense of balance and cohesion.

As far as table settings are concerned, the best way to achieve a tasteful ambience is to let the food do the talking. If your eating area is of the Zen minimalist variety, try matching a crisp white linen tablecloth with plain, upholstered chairs in order to create an enticingly pristine canvas. By the same token, keep your implements simple: fine bone china in white or cream, simple uncut tumblers (rather than traditional stemware) and clear acrylic resin cutlery will achieve a cool and contemporary look.

In order to promote an organic feel in a rustic eating space, you should either leave your tabletop bare or cover it with a tablecloth made from rough-and-ready hessian. Alternatively, mark each place setting with mats made from raffia, bamboo or cork, and furnish them with oversized wooden platters, chunky peasant-style pottery, bamboo-handled cutlery and heavy stone candlesticks. By the same token, fussier items such as napkin rings are a definite no-no; instead, simply fold napkins in half or tie them with a length of raffia, which is as effective as it is aesthetically pleasing.

The subtle contrast of pattern, texture and size is another important feature of table display. For example, add interest to an all-white table by laying it with a gloriously interwoven damask tablecloth – and highlight the effect by using clear-glass plates. Alternatively, contrast a textured tablecloth with smooth wooden beakers, or ground an

Not only does the simplicity of the monochrome setting (below) make a dramatic statement, but it also enables the diner to concentrate on the pleasure of eating and drinking, free from the encumbrance of rows of cutlery and stacks of crockery.

A plain but elegant table should be the main focus of your eating area (this page). **Opt for a wood or stone design to help create a solid central feature, and surround with chairs that are uniformly simple, as well as being comfortable, so your guests will want to linger over their food.**

It is possible to create subtle layers of interest within your table settings through pattern and texture. The mix of antique tumblers and goblets (bottom right) is offset by the interwoven design of the damask tablecloth, while different-patterned napkins (below right) maintain a cohesive feel by sticking to a two-tone colour scheme.

One of the simplest and most effective ways to create a calming atmosphere in your eating space is to opt for matching table and chairs (opposite). By doing this, you can choose a more intricate design, while still maintaining an uncluttered and cohesive feel.

essentially ephemeral display by adding chunky candle blocks. It is also possible to mix patterns without the overall effect appearing too busy, as long as you stick to a simple palette of two colours. Although the tabletop should be kept simple, decorative details still have a part to play: a brace of potted orchids, a scattering of petals or a cluster of votive candles all promote a dreamlike quality, while a bowl of textured fruit and vegetables (such as white gourds, artichokes and quinces) adds a sculptural look.

FEED THE BODY, NOURISH THE SOUL
Due to the evocative effect of food aromas and tastes on the psyche, the foods we cook play an important role in the atmosphere of the home. Smells such as freshly roasted coffee, bread rising in the oven, or the sticky aroma of toffee can all provoke vivid memories, such as a holiday on the continent or childhood visits to the fair. In addition, the sweet smell of chocolate has a particularly powerful effect, boosting serotonin levels in the brain before it even enters our digestive system. The spiritual kitchen is not a place of abstinence – so tuck in!

Keep your sleeping space simple. Reduce furniture to the
bare minimum; adopt a cohesive colour scheme; and rely
on space, light and texture to create a sensory haven.

sleeping

The Zen philosophy of preserving a calm physical space
in order to clear the mind is a particularly pertinent one
when it comes to the spiritual bedroom. Demanding the
kind of hallowed atmosphere that emanates from an inner
sanctum, the ethos blends comfort with minimalism in
order to boost mental and physical health.

In these days of high-stress jobs and hectic lifestyles,
lack of sleep is a pressing preoccupation. Due to the ever-
increasing demands of modern life, many of us are simply
not clocking up enough ZZZs to keep body and soul
together. But sleep is not just about quantity – it's also
about quality. If our bedrooms are too hot or too cold, too
cluttered or too noisy, our sleep will be seriously affected.
The answer is to keep things simple and to ban all
distracting detritus from the room. The bed itself should
be a island of relaxation, so prune the rest of your
furniture and furnishings accordingly. Nothing should
detract from the sensory delights of this room – the
ultimate comfort zone of your home.

A PLACE TO DREAM
Choosing a bed is one of the most important decisions you
will make when it comes to kitting out your space. Not
only does a good night's sleep help to restore our spirits,

99

but creating a comfy nest is also of prime importance when you consider that we spend one third of our lives curled up under the duvet. As a result, purchasing a quality mattress is key to promoting the most effective downtime possible. Whether you choose to sleep in a romantic sleigh bed, a grand four-poster, or something altogether more modern and minimal, your bed should be large enough – and luxurious enough – to spend the weekend in.

COSMIC COLOUR PALETTES

White is the ideal colour for the spiritual bedroom. Representing cleanliness and peace, it is also cool and contemporary, and promotes a serene sense of coherence that is conducive to relaxation. Opting for an all-white bedroom does not, however, mean you must sleep in a stark monastic cube. Instead, apply tinted paints to give your walls a warm glow; juxtapose textures and shapes to create interest; and use lighting – natural and artificial – to achieve pattern and depth. A white room also provides the ideal canvas for the occasional flick of colour or splash of

Far from being cold, the serene palette of the blue bedroom (above and right) **is ultimately restful on the eye. The soft honey tones of the woodwork and the throw at the end of the bed provide a calming complement to the collection of similar-style pictures propped in a haphazard fashion behind the pillows.**

In order to accommodate the pattern and texture of the log-cabin walls, the furnishings in the bedroom (opposite) **are kept to a minimum without causing the overall effect to appear too spartan. Rather, the simple white bedlinen gives a cosy feel, while the anglepoise lamp adds a chic urban twist.**

pattern; drape a turquoise throw across snowy white sheets, for example, or top a standard lamp with a hot pink shade. Alternatively, throw a scarlet kimono across the foot of the bed or snuggle up under a colourful antique patchwork quilt.

If white is too clinical for you, earthy neutrals in shades of buff, beige or biscuit, or soothing shades of blue, green, yellow, grey and pink, will also give a calming feel. Anyone suffering from insomnia should opt for blue or violet – the two most spiritual colours in the spectrum, which have been been proved to lower blood pressure and to promote peaceful feelings.

TURN ON, CHILL OUT

Because it has such a strong impact on mood, it is important to get the lighting of your bedroom just right. Natural light nourishes our souls, while the artificial illuminations that supplement it, such as the gentle glow from a bedside lamp, should help you to unwind. If

By keeping basic furnishings in the bedroom to a minimum, it is possible to introduce a bold mix of pattern and colour (above). By the same token, the bare white walls and stark design of the bed (opposite, above left and below) allows for a dramatic red-and-white colour scheme – from the painted woodwork, through the simple checks of the curtains, to the embroidered pattern of the Shaker-style quilts.

A mix of fabrics, in florals, stripes and checks, on the sleigh bed (opposite, right) creates a pretty and uncontrived look in a country bedroom that is otherwise almost entirely stripped of furnishings.

One of the best ways to enhance light and space in the bedroom is to opt for a cheerful colour scheme. The yellow and white palette in the space (left) is a perfect example of this, helping to open out the room and prevent the patchwork quilt and drawer-lined wall from appearing too busy.

think of your bed as a remote island floating in a calm sea

possible, sleep in a room that faces east. This way you will benefit from the galvanizing energy of the morning sun, which provides the necessary impetus to get out of bed. That said, a harsh glare can be invasive, so opt for blinds or curtains made from light-filtering fabrics such as voile or muslin. An advantage of floaty drapes is their ability to emphasize the movement of air, which will also help to enhance a spiritually ephemeral feel.

Artificial lighting should be soft and relaxing. Mix ambient illuminations and specific task lights (essential for reading), in order to create an intimate glow that is conducive to sleep. In addition, make sure that your light levels are adjustable, as hard bright light in a minimalist space can make it seem cold and clinical. Instead, opt

The neutral palette in the bedroom (below) is prevented from becoming too impersonal by the floaty pink drapes at the window and the spray of flowers on the bedside table.

A stainless-steel trolley, pink curtains and Moroccan slippers in the bedroom (right) create a lighthearted quirky feel, although the overall ambience is a restful one.

The grandeur of the carved bed (opposite) is complemented by a brace of navy lampshades, while the soft woollen throws are soothing against the coarse canework of the bed frame.

The intricate design of the wrought-iron bed (below) is calm and serene thanks to its elegant proportions and the plain bedlinen. The spindly legs of the furnishings – which seem to float above the floor – are countered by the bare wooden boards.

for indirect lighting that has a two-tone effect – creating pools of warmth on walls and ceilings, while leaving other areas of the room mysteriously shadowy.

UNASHAMEDLY LUXURIOUS FABRICS

Although the spiritual bedroom is fundamentally minimalist in style, it is not in any way austere. Choose linens and silks to usher in a mood of sensuality, and make your bed a key site for the creation of a simply sybaritic style.

We all know the feeling of bliss that comes from climbing between fresh sheets that have been aired and scented. The sensation of natural fabrics on your bare skin is one of the best soul-soothers in the world, while falling back on freshly plumped pillows helps to ease away the stresses and strains of the day. As a result, it is vitally important that your bedlinen is made from high-quality, natural fibres. (It goes without saying that the peaceful bedroom is a pure-cotton, rather than a polycotton, kind of place.)

If your sleeping area is a symphony in white, then pristine bedlinen is a must. Thankfully, there are numerous different styles of plain bed dressings on the market, allowing for the creation of interest within the confines of a minimalist palette. For example, contrast stark white sheets with a sumptuous satin comforter, or combine delicately detailed fabrics such as lace and *broderie anglaise* with more robust ones like waffle-weave or wool. A dove-white bed can also be enhanced by the addition of floaty drapes falling from a

A combination of pink and white creates a calming colour scheme (opposite), while the dark metal spindles of the bedhead help to anchor the look and prevent it from appearing too ephemeral.

The slippery sheen of the bedcover (left) contrasts with the stark lines of the bench, slatted chair and anglepoise lamp, in order to create a pleasing balance between luxury and rigour.

choose sheets in calming colours, and contrast textures and styles to prevent your sleeping space appearing bland

Semi-opaque glass bricks, lilac walls and a beechwood Bunny chair lift the monastic-looking bedroom (left) out of the ordinary and give it a funky new twist.

The cream-painted panelling and bed (above) create a cosy reassuring feel, while the crisp cotton pillows and plain bedside table complete the look, which is fresh and inviting.

107

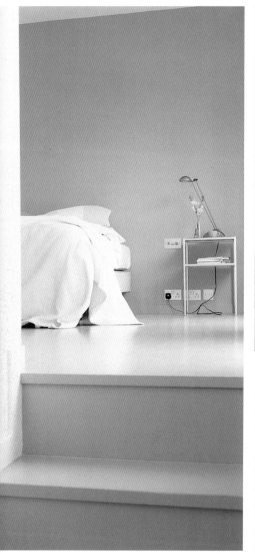

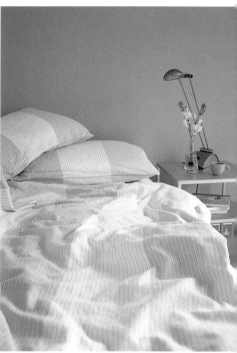

corona attached to the ceiling. In this way, you can turn your bed into a seductive haven of dreams and romance.

Bedrooms decorated in a range of neutral colours also provide a variety of options in terms of tactile choice. Organic materials such as alpaca, hessian and linen tone well with wooden beds, while a warm mix of luxurious textures promotes a reassuring grounded feel. Take your pick from brushed cotton, cashmere, suede, angora or mohair.

Far from being grey and depressing, the sophisticated colour scheme in the bedroom (opposite) **provides a calming antidote to the chaos of colour and clutter of the outside world; instead, the look is crisp and light.**

A scatter of cushions is one of the quickest ways to soften the starkness of an all-white bedroom (left). **Here, the simple colour scheme of brown and white allows for the introduction of different patterns and textures, without creating a conflict of interest.**

A raw linen cushion cover (below) **has a pleasing texture, its coarse fibres contrasting with its soft functionalism.**

SLEEPY SCENTS

Said to promote physical, mental and spiritual well-being, lavender is one of the best known cures for insomnia. Administer it by spritzing your sheets with lavender water or by putting a couple of drops of lavender essential oil onto your pillow. If symptoms persist, step up your campaign by slipping a lavender bag into your pillowcase or hot-water-bottle cover, and keep a bowl of dried lavender on your bedside table.

The best way to create a peaceful washing space is to keep the fixtures and fittings in your bathroom simple. Taps should be plumbed into the wall (opposite) to keep bath and basin edges clear, while industrial building materials such as concrete and glass (left) offer an attractive and durable alternative to the bathroom 'suite'.

bathing

Since the 1950s, the bathroom has metamorphosed from a washing space into a haven of relaxation and pampering.

The development of the bathroom from a functional place of ablutions reflects a growing interest in our mental and spiritual health, and takes its cue from traditional Japanese bath-house design, which focuses on water therapy as an effective way to soothe the soul. As a result, Western bathrooms are becoming increasingly like spas in order to recreate a similarly serene feel. Fixtures and fittings blend seamlessly with the overall decor; colour is reduced to one or two shades; and ugly pipes are boxed away. In this way, we can concentrate on the ritual of purification without becoming distracted by visual detritus.

CLEANSE THE SPACE, PURIFY THE SOUL
Keeping your bathroom simple demands the adoption of a strict minimalist code. Plumb taps into a facing wall so that bath and basin edges remain clear, and replace cosmetic-laden shelves with unobtrusive cabinets.

111

Decorative accessories, too, should be kept to a minimum: a single picture or potted palm may be enough if spiritual rejuvenation is your main aim. If you feel the need for a greater display of personal accessories in your bathing space, stick to natural objects, focusing on textural contrast rather than harsh colours.

SLEEK SURFACE TREATMENTS

Although the spiritual bathroom is an essentially minimalist space, this does not mean there is a lack of choice when it comes to surface treatments. Rather, there are myriad finishes available – from smooth ceramics to gleaming stainless steel, patterned marbles to cool glass, and warm woods to tinted concrete.

If your washing space has an earthy organic theme, then a soft wooden finish is advised. Not only does timber look great against a backdrop of calming neutrals but, if you choose a hardwearing variety

With today's emphasis on water therapy as an effective salve for the soul, bathrooms are becoming increasingly minimalist, taking inspiration from modern spas (opposite). **Colours are clean and cool, and furnishings and fittings pruned to the bare essentials.**

A softer feel can be created with the use of warm colours and interesting textures (above); **likewise, a display of crystals is decorative without appearing overly fussy** (above left).

112

Although it is pared down, the washing space (opposite and left) **has a warm earthy feel thanks to a rattan storage selection and the soft circle of the basin. A couple of sea sponges and a simple vase of flowers complete the organic look.**

shades of white or cream provide a pristine backdrop in which to cleanse body and soul

Whether you choose a boxy Japanese-style tub or an antique roll-top one (below), **your bath should be long enough and deep enough for a seriously good wallow – a place where you can read, meditate or enjoy a calming cup of herbal tea.**

that has been treated to resist water, you can also use it for fixtures and fittings such as your bath, basin and toilet. Favoured by the Japanese for hundreds of years, a timber tub offers a wonderfully elemental bathing experience – combining a warm tactile feel with the fabulous aroma of wood, which is released when your bath fills with hot water.

Stone is another effective treatment in the bathroom, providing a feeling of immutability that contrasts with the edgy hi-tech world outside. Like wood, stone is tough, durable and water-resistant. It is available in a wide variety of types and finishes: choose granite if you want to create a macho urban feel or soft sandstone for a warmer, earthier look. It is also possible to opt for super-deluxe marble – this once impossibly expensive stone is now more cheaply available in the form of tiles, veneers and marble-and-resin composites. Alternatively, opt for cast concrete, which is now as popular indoors as it is out. Mixed to

a number of specialist finishes, concrete can match much of the sensual appeal of stone – its texture and colour manipulated to produce a variety of pleasing results.

SIMPLE SHADES

One of the best ways to create a cleansing ambience in the bathroom is to keep your palette to a minimum of one or two colours. It doesn't matter what shades you choose as long as they are clear and tonal (strong, dense colours are likely to restrain, rather than free, the spirit). Shades of white or cream are ideal, providing a clear, light feel – unlike the ubiquitous 1970s avocado suite, which has rapidly fallen from grace.

This watery room is the perfect place to mix reflective surfaces. The smoked-glass shelf, shiny basin and chrome fixtures (left) fit the bill nicely, and contrast with the fissured strata of the limestone wall tiles.

Expensive designer lotions and potions have no place in the peaceful bathing space. Instead, the look is natural and organic, relying instead on simple soaps and plain cotton towels (above) for maximum effect.

The soft sandstone of the bathroom (opposite) creates a warm earthy feel, while the niche position of the tub compounds the sense of sanctuary.

Thanks to its associations with the sea and sky, blue also works well in the spiritual bathroom. Light variations of this watery shade will help to calm the body and still the mind. In addition, blue provides the perfect complement to white, while the combination of these two colours gives an appropriate seaside feel and prevents your space from appearing too clinical.

For a calming back-to-basics look that is more homely than spa-like, choose a neutral palette in muted earth

colours. Soft greens, pale browns and sandy yellows all give a natural grounded effect, as well as providing the perfect complement to surfaces such as stone and wood. In addition, a neutral palette provides the ideal backdrop for organic accessories such as sisal baskets, loofahs, seashells and natural sponges.

CALM REFLECTIONS

The elemental aspect of bathing means that light is an important aspect in the bathroom, helping to compound our connection with the natural world. As a result, many modern bathrooms are designed to harness as much

A grey-brown limestone, mottled with fossil remains, is saved from being overly cool and dark (left) by the warm-toned slatted blinds and the wall length of mirrored cabinets, which help to bounce light back into the room. Further contrast is provided by the vertical ribbing cut into the bath surround and walls.

Reflective surfaces such as chrome and shiny ceramics (above and right) are another way to make your bathroom appear lighter and brighter, especially if your colour scheme revolves around dark and dramatic stone.

Attaining a truly peaceful bathroom demands a strict code: fixtures and fittings should blend seamlessly with the overall decor; colour should be limited to one or two shades; and the visual distraction of decorative elements kept to a minimum.

light as possible – either through the addition of extra windows or via a skylight positioned directly above your washing area. In this way, bathers can enjoy the great outdoors through the contemplation of clouds, treetops and birds in flight as they lie back in the tub.

If your wash space is the pristine all-white variety, reinforced glass is the ideal complement, helping to imbue the space with a light, ephemeral feel. Glass is extremely versatile, durable and easy to clean, as well as being available in a variety of forms – including plain, opaque, coloured and frosted. Use it for walls, doors and screens, or in the construction of a shower cubicle, basin or bath.

It is also possible to make your bathroom appear bigger and brighter through the use of artfully placed mirrors, which bounce light back into the room. In addition, reflective glass can be used to create alternative dimensions, offering bathers the magical sensation of wallowing in an illusory space.

soothing sense of continuity in the washing space (far left and left), connecting bath, basin and shower cubicle with total fluidity. In addition, their circular shape creates a calming antidote to the rigid lines of the wall tiles.

A shiny rubber floor and long elegant bath give the washing space (below) an almost monastic appearance.

A series of identically placed windows and carefully positioned mirrors provide a

a pristine space allows you to concentrate on the ritual of purification

SOOTHING LOTIONS, POTIONS AND ACCESSORIES
In a truly spiritual bathing space, cosmetic items should be hidden from sight. Evidence of the mundane essentials needed to keep body and soul together will destroy the soothing ambience of the room, so ensure that toothpaste, razors and cotton-wool balls are neatly stowed in a streamlined cabinet.

It is acceptable, however, to display a few essential unguents. Decant shampoo, conditioner, shower gel and bath oils into spiritually aesthetic bottles, and make a display of organic soap, sea sponges and loofahs – all of which add an earthy elemental feel. Plants also work well in the spiritual bathroom, absorbing extra humidity and making your space feel fresh and alive. The occasional frondy fern will help to soften hard angular surfaces, while plants with scented flowers will add a delicate fragrance – orchids are a particular favourite, as they thrive in a humid atmosphere and add an exotic, mystical feel.

121

The customized Eames chair and velvet cushion are a far cry from the dull uniformity of office furniture, while tin cans, which have been stripped of their labels, add a dash of fashionable eco-chic.

Whether you plan to work from home full time, or simply want to create an 'admin' area where you can write letters and catch up on your paperwork, it is vital that you create an organized space in which to focus the mind.

working

In the space of a single generation, communications technology has revolutionized our working lives. Thanks to the advent of email and the internet, we can now dispatch the printed word at the touch of a button, glean information on any given subject in minutes and communicate with people on the other side of the world at a fraction of the cost of a telephone call. As a result, an increasing number of people are working from home – relying on computer technology to keep them in touch with the outside world. This arrangement is particularly effective for those seeking a peaceful working environment in which to nurture mind, body and soul. In addition, working from home also offers an escape route from the irritations of office life, where ringing phones, harassed colleagues, endless meetings and the daily commute to and from work all fray our nerves and deplete our spiritual reserves.

ORGANIZING YOUR WORK ETHICS

Your workspace should be designed to cater for the work you want to achieve – be it negotiating a complex business deal, writing a book, designing a website or simply sorting out your accounts. Without doubt, you will perform much more efficiently if you have a well-ordered, comfortable and visually appealing place to do this in.

It is also important that you invest time and money in the creation of a conducive working environment, as any initial outlay will quickly be repaid in terms of increased productivity. As a result, consider the conversion potential of any spare space in your home – the attic, a roomy walk-in cupboard or the conservatory, for example. Alternatively, build a workstation

It is not necessary to set aside a whole room in order to create an effective work area. Instead, the cleverly compact office unit (left) tucks neatly into a corner and incorporates enough space for a computer, printer and fax without appearing overbearing. In addition, its light, bright and uplifting colour scheme is conducive to creativity.

Although starkly minimalist in appearance, a good deal of thought has gone into the design of the office (opposite, right) – from the practicality of the cantilevered adjustable desk lamp designed by Richard Sapper to the solidity of the old wooden desk. The result is an effective workspace that is both comfortable and aesthetic.

If your work creates volumes of paperwork, a wall of built-in units (below and right) will provide ample storage space. Ensure that your cupboards are big enough to accommodate bulky box files.

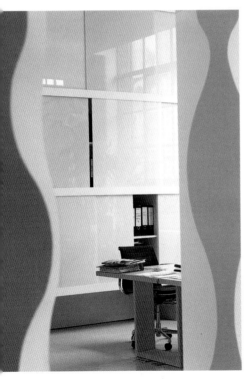

into the corner of an underused room, such as a dining room or spare bedroom.

DIVINE DECOR INSPIRATION

One of the best aspects of working from home is the exhilarating liberation from standard office furnishings. While elephant-grey desks, brooding computers and institutionalized carpeting are a fact of life in offices across the world, the home office is a much more aesthetic affair, individually designed to reflect the personality of its occupant and effect first-rate results.

The most effective workspace is simple but slick – relying on a handful of furnishings for an uncluttered environment where ideas can flow freely. Once again, a pale palette is best for promoting clarity of thought, with neutrals such as stone, ivory and string coming top of the class for creating a contemplative feel. Alternatively, opt for clear tones such as duck-egg blue or primrose yellow, against which a modern print or a jewel-bright chair will create an inspiring focal point.

A bright red chair adds a cheerful note to the simple workstation (opposite), while the natural light that streams through the big window imbues the businesslike environment with an upbeat positive feel.

A smattering of funky additions creates a personalized charm which, in turn, aids creativity. A black-and-white photograph, vase and modern floor light (above right) **soften the hard lines of the industrial workspace, as well as helping to counter the harsh urban view.**

The furnishings for a home office should be chosen carefully. Good-quality, sturdy storage solutions (above left) **will repay you in years of service. Make sure, too, that your workstation is always properly illuminated – adjustable lamps are ideal for this** (above).

Good lighting is also important in the home office. If possible, place your workstation near a window, as natural light aids creativity. As far as artificial illumination is concerned, make sure that an anglepoise lamp is an integral feature of your desk.

SITTING PRETTY

Your desk and chair are the most important purchases you will make when setting up a home office. Even if your budget is limited, it is vital that you spend time and money sourcing the best ergonomic designs available, as this will protect you against debilitating conditions such as low back pain and repetitive strain injury.

127

Start off by choosing a desk that is large enough to accommodate your computer, mouse mat, phone and in-tray, without cramping your style. If your work demands creativity, source a round desk which will encourage original thoughts and ideas. By contrast, if your business involves working with numbers, a conventional rectangular or square desk is a better choice.

As far as chairs are concerned, choose an adjustable style which will provide good lower back support – this is vital if you intend to spend long periods sitting at your desk. Chairs on castors are another good idea, as they allow for flexible movement around the work area.

One of the perks of working from home is liberation from grungey office furnishings. The simple wooden trestle table (above) creates ample space for catching up on paperwork, while the gingham-covered chair gives a cheerful lift. In addition, a white-painted filing cabinet blends seamlessly into the space, while the aroma from the pot of rosemary helps to promote clarity of thought.

POSITIVE VIBES AND STIMULATING SCENTS
To work at peak efficiency, you need to create a stimulating atmosphere. One of the best ways to achieve this is by investing in an ionizer to combat toxic computer emissions. Place a couple of leafy plants, also known for their air-purifying abilities, near your computer to compound the effect.

Aromatherapy is another good way of providing an invigorating work environment. The following fragrances are known for their mind-enhancing properties: for clarity of thought, choose rosemary or basil; to counteract mental fatigue, basil; to stimulate the brain, eucalyptus or sage; to boost memory, ginger, basil, lemon, grapefruit, rosemary, coriander or peppermint; and for creative inspiration, frankincense, bergamot, rose, jasmine or cinnamon.

If you suffer from lack of concentration, light a candle (left). Not only will the flame provide a calming focal point, but the scent of aromatherapy candles can also help to kickstart the brain. Flowers and herbs are similarly stimulating; choose mint as a powerful aid to concentration.

It is not necessary to opt for a standard desk and chair in order to create an effective workspace. As long as your chair is at the right height for your desk, it is possible to choose a variety of different furnishing styles. A café chair combined with an old sewing-machine table (this page) provides a good set up for writing the odd letter, while a comfy armchair is ideal for flicking through magazines.

A glass wall overlooking a calm expanse of water creates a peaceful vista for the occupants of this house. Not only does the seamless transition between outside and in provide a connection with nature, but the reflective quality of the water is also meditative and restful.

outdoor living

You needn't live in a country retreat with big sweeping lawns in order to create a tranquil space where you can touch the earth and feel the air.

In the same way that plants wither and die from lack of light, so the human psyche shrivels when it is deprived of contact with the rhythms of the earth. As a result, it is vital that our environments include an area where we can benefit from the healing power of nature.

It doesn't matter whether your exterior space consists of a vast rambling garden or a concrete balcony the size of a handkerchief – or even if you have no outdoor space at all. What is important is that you create a tranquil retreat where you can reconnect with mother earth. By committing yourself to the loving maintenance of your garden – or to bringing the outdoors into your home – you will create the optimum conditions for your spirituality to flourish and grow.

BLURRING THE BOUNDARIES
The importance of connecting with the natural world cannot be over-emphasized in the home. Even if you have a generous-sized garden, it is still necessary to establish a link between your interior space and your exterior one. The best way to blur the boundaries is to install floor-to-

131

The calming space of the bedroom
(right) has been enhanced by the
simple balcony accessed through
French windows. Not only does this
provide increased light and space,
but the view of sky and treetops is
supremely restorative.

An indoor pond has been created
amidst the stone and concrete
confines of a converted warehouse
(below). The design is based on the
peaceful premise of a Zen garden,
including the addition of a large
boulder as part of the pond wall.
However, the contemporary setting
gives a quirky twist and yanks the
look into the twenty-first century.

Converted from a former dairy barn,
the elegant lap pool (opposite) has
been painted bright white to
resemble a boathouse. A collection
of floating balls increases the
feeling of tranquillity and reflection.

ceiling sliding glass doors and to maintain the same
floor surface either side. If you have no outside space
whatsoever, it does not mean you need to feel isolated
from nature. Instead, combine elements such as skylights,
plants and water features to create an indoor 'garden'.

CREATING A ZEN GARDEN OF NATURAL HARMONY

One of the most effective ways to 'spiritualize' an outside
space is to imitate the Zen gardens of old and to arrange
stones, shrubs, water, trees and sand to create an
energizing balance of yin and yang. However, it is not
necessary to adhere to a rigorous Japanese design in
order to create a tranquil space. As long as clutter is kept
to a minimum and natural materials are used, it is
possible to promote feelings of serenity through the
addition of a few key features. For example, if you have
a small back yard, use silvery wooden decking, gravel or
simple stone flags to create a calming, grounded feel.
Alternatively, pave your space with tinted concrete and
add wispy ornamental grasses to soften the effect. It is

Even if your outside area is the size of a pocket handkerchief, it is possible to create a natural haven by dint of lateral thinking. The wooden slatted screen (opposite) creates an ordered sense of Zen tranquillity, while the lush foliage overhanging it softens the look. By the same token, the plain bench running alongside provides conducive seating, thanks to the welcome addition of a single cushion.

A tiny city roof terrace (left) – with the addition of wooden decking, a couple of cosy wicker chairs and a selection of cheerful tubs – is all it takes to commune with the natural world.

If you have no access to an outside space, it is still perfectly possible to create a similar feel indoors. The generous-sized skylight, stone-flagged floor and a foliage-filled hanging basket (above) give a natural airy look.

also possible to make your outside space more peaceful through the addition of furniture and accessories in calming shapes and interesting textures. For instance, a trio of differently sized stone balls will create a soothing focal point, while a simple wood bench (preferably placed in the shade of an ancient tree) presents the perfect meditation spot. Cane or bamboo chairs also compound the elemental look, as do portable lanterns in hammered steel.

GO GREEN WITH NON-FLOWERING PLANTS
Although aroma is a key feature in the home, the presence of fragrant flowers is not integral to the creation of a soulful outside space. Instead, tall grasses and leafy plants take

centre stage by emphasizing the all-green cohesion and calm of Zen garden design.

In addition to being fashionable, wispy greenery is also gratifyingly easy to care for. Choose from fast-growing golden or black bamboo – which introduces movement and height – or the swaying grace of ornamental grasses, which quiver even in the lightest of breezes. Alternatively, if you want a graphic look, fill smooth silver planters with succulents and surround them with artful pebble arrangements. Pots of blue-green *Helictotrichon* grass also work well, promoting

feelings of vibrancy and health, while the feathery foliage of silver- and grey-leafed plants introduces a subtle colour contrast.

WATER, STAFF OF LIFE

Known for its remedial properties, the cleansing essence of water has been used in religious practices for thousands of years. Accordingly, water helps to still our minds and allow our thoughts to ascend to a higher plane. Introduce water to your outside area through the addition of a spouting fountain or a glassy pond – both are highly effective ways to quieten the mind and promote feelings of reflection. Moving water is dynamic, vibrant and alive. Not only does its lyrical movement induce spiritual calm, but the appearance of running water also frees our creativity and helps us to think more spontaneously. In Zen philosophy, it is thought to carry chi – the energizing force essential for life. By contrast, still water is quiet, tranquil and serene; its reflective qualities help to expand our horizons, while its glassy depths aid meditation. If you have a pond, enhance spiritual feelings by adding water lilies – which represent purity and decency according to Zen beliefs – and fish, which the dictates of feng shui say will augur health and prosperity.

If your outside space is limited to just a small area, create a mini water feature by covering the base of a large glass bowl or vase with pebbles and filling it with water. Float a flower head or candle on the surface, to highlight the soothing ripples produced by natural air currents.

Vital for inducing feelings of tranquillity, water is a key feature in the creation of a peaceful outside space. Whether you opt for the mellifluous sound of water falling from a spout (above)**, or the meditative depths of a still-water pond, is up to you.**

A wooden deck (opposite) **large enough for a table and chairs is the ideal way to enjoy the outdoors. Choose natural materials and simple furnishings that will blend harmoniously with the surrounding environs.**

picture credits

Key: a=above, b=below, l=left, r=right, c=centre

ARCHITECTS AND DESIGNERS WHOSE WORK IS FEATURED IN THIS BOOK:

Asfour Guzy
594 Broadway, # 1204
New York, NY 10012
USA
+1 212 334 9350
Page 17

Ash Sakula Architects
24 Rosebery Avenue
London EC1R 4SX
020 7837 9735
www.ashsak.com
Pages 79, 89

Azman Associates
(formerly Azman Owens Architects)
18 Charlotte Road
London EC2A 3PB
020 7739 8191
www.azmanowens.com
Page 78l&r

Babylon Design Ltd
Lighting Designers
301 Fulham Road
London SW10 9QH
020 7376 7233
www.babylonlondon.com
Pages 125l & r, 127r

Barefoot Elegance
Dot Spikings and
Jennifer Castle
3537 Old Conejo Road,
Suite 105
Newbury Park,
CA 91320
USA
+1 805 499 5959
Pages 12–13, 30, 33r, 38r, 43

JoAnn Barwick
Interior Designer
P.O. Box 982
Boca Grande,
FL 33921
USA
Pages 83br, 103r

Claire Bataille & Paul ibens
Design NV
Architects
Vekestratt 13 Bus 14
2000 Antwerp
Belgium
+32 3 231 3593
Pages 80–81, 118–119, 119b

Bedmar & Shi Designers Pte Ltd
12a Keong Saik Road
Singapore 089119
+65 22 77117
bedmar.shi@
  pacific.net.sg
Pages 97, 136

Belmont Freeman Architects
110 West 40th Street
New York, NY 10018
USA
+1 212 382 3311
Page 126

Laura Bohn Design Associates, Inc.
30 West 26th Street
New York, NY 10010
USA
+1 212 645 3636
Page 135r

Bowles & Linares
32 Hereford Road
London W2 5AJ
020 7229 9886
Page 93

Ann Boyd Design Ltd
33 Elystan Street
London SW3 3NT
020 7591 0202
Page 41

Nancy Braithwaite Interiors
2300 Peachtree Road,
Suite C101
Atlanta, GA 30309
USA
Pages 18, 51

Cabot Design Ltd
Interior Design
1925 Seventh Avenue,
Suite 71
New York, NY 10026
USA
+1 212 222 9488
eocabot@aol.com
Page 55

Circus Architects
Unit 111
The Foundry
165 Blackfriars Road
London SE1 8EN
020 7953 7322
Page 90

Conner Prairie Museum
13400 Alisonville Road
Fishers, IN 46038
USA
Pages 10–11,102a

Damien D'Arcy Associates
9 Lamington Street
London W6 0HU
020 8741 1193
Page 113

De Le Cuona Textile and Home Collection
9–10 Osborne Mews
Windsor SL4 3DE
01753 830301
www.delecuona.co.uk
Pages 62, 63l

De Metz Architects
Unit 4, 250 Finchley Road
London NW3 6DN
020 7435 1144
Page 23

Terry Dorrough
Architect
14 Riverview Avenue
Dangar Island
NSW 2083
Australia
+61 2 9985 7729
Page 134

Robert Dye Associates
Design Consultants/
Chartered Architects
Linton House
39–51 Highgate Road
London NW5 1RS
020 7267 9388
www.robertdye.com
Page 100

Jamie Falla
MooArc
198 Blackstock Road
London N5 1EN
020 7345 1729
www.mooarc.com
Page 53a

Featherstone Associates
74 Clerkenwell Road
London EC1M 5QA
020 7490 1212
www.featherstone-
associates.co.uk
Page 121b

Han Feng
Fashion Designer
333 West 39th Street,
12th Floor
New York, NY 10018
USA
+1 212 695 9509
Page 61

Ken Foreman
Architect
105 Duane Street
New York, NY 10007
USA
+1 212 924 4503
Page 112r

Zina Glazebrook
ZG Design
Bridgehampton, NY
+1 631 537 4454
www.zgdesign.com
Pages 24, 133

Glomdalsmueet
Museum for Østerdalen
and Solar
2400 Elverum
Norway
Page 57l

Mark Guard Architects
161 Whitfield Street
London W1P 5RY
020 7380 1199
Pages 98–99

Alastair Hendy
Food Writer, Art
Director and Designer
fax 020 7739 6040
Pages 2, 8–9, 60

John C. Hope Architects
3 St Bernard's
Crescent
Edinburgh EH4 1NR
0131 315 2215
Page 15

Jacomini Interior Design
1701 Brun, Suite 101
Houston, TX 77019
USA
Pages 83 al, 103al&bl

Joanna Jefferson Architects
222 Oving Road
Chichester
West Sussex
PO19 4EJ
01243 532398
jjeffearch@aol.com
Pages 70–71

Just Design Ltd
80 Fifth Avenue,
18th Floor
New York, NY 10011
USA
+1 212 243 6544
www.justdesignltd.com
Page 25

Kayode Lipede
020 7794 7535
Page 90

**James Lynch, D.A.D.
Associates**
112–116 Old Street
London EC1V 9BG
Page 36

Hilton McConnico
Interior Home Designer
8 rue Antoine Panier
93170 Bagnolet
France
+33 1 43 62 53 16
hmc@club-internet.fr
Page 121al&ar

Ocke Mannerfelt
Architect
Hamnvägen 8
S-18351 Täby
Sweden
Pages 50–51

**David Mikhail
Architects**
68–74 Rochester Place
London NW1 9JX
020 7485 4696
www.dmikhail.
freeserve.co.uk
Page 119a

L.A. Morgan
Interior Designer
P.O. Box 39
Hadlyme, CT 06439
USA
+1 860 434 0304
Page 42b

**Mullman Seidman
Architects**
443 Greenwich Street
New York, NY 10013
USA
+1 212 431 0770
www.mullman
seidman.com
Page 54b

Roger Oates Design
01531 631611
www.rogeroates.co.uk
*Pages 16, 58c, 58r,
104l*

Orefelt Associates
43 Pall Mall Deposit
124–128 Barlby Road
London W10 6BL
020 8960 2560
Pages 110, 111

**Graham Phillips
RIBA**
Architect
Pages 3br, 130–131

**Mathew Priestman
Architects**
6–8 Emerald Street
London WC1N 3QA
020 7404 3113
Front jacket

Potted Gardens
27 Bedford Street
New York, NY 10014
USA
Page 82

Lena Proudlock
Denim in Style
25a Long Street
Tetbury GL8 8AA
www.deniminstyle.com
Page 20

**Reed Creative
Services Ltd**
151a Sydney Street
London SW3 6NT
020 7565 0066
Page 29bl

Les Reedman
Chartered Architect/
Architectural Historian
P.O. Box 148
Brooklyn, NSW 2083
Australia
+61 2 9985 7893
Page 137

**Nico Rensch
Architeam**
www.architeam.co.uk
01424 445885
Page 109l

Johanne Riss
Stylist, Designer and
Fashion Designer
35 Place du Nouveau
Marché aux Graens
1000 Bruxelles
Belgium
+32 2 513 0900
www.johanneriss.com
Page 132b

Jim Ruscitto
Ruscitto, Latham,
Blanton Architects
P.O. Box 419
Sun Valley, ID 83353
USA
Pages 48, 57, 101

SCDA Architects
10 Teck Lim Road
Singapore 088386
+65 324 5458
scda@cyberway.
com.sg
Page 116l

Sheila Scholes
Designer
01480 498241
Page 84al

**Johnson
Schwinghammer**
339 West 38th Street,
#9
New York, NY 10018
USA
+1 212 643 1552
Pages 3al, 29al, 75

Sequana
64 avenue de la Motte
Picquet
75015 Paris, France
+33 1 45 66 58 40
sequana@wandoo.fr
Page 64a

**Shelton, Mindel &
Associates**
216 West 18th Street
New York, NY 10011
USA
+1 212 243 3939
Pages 3al, 29al, 75

**Square Foot
Properties Ltd**
50 Britton Street
London EC1M 5UP
020 7253 2527
Page 107bl

Guy Stansfeld
020 8962 8666
Pages 14br, 112l

Seth Stein
15 Grand Union Centre
West Row
London W10 5AS
020 8968 8581
Page 95

**Stickland Coombe
Architecture**
258 Lavender Hill
London SW11 1LJ
020 7924 1699
nick@scadesign.
freeserve.co.uk
Pages 108, 120

Sally Storey
John Cullen Lighting
585 King's Road
London SW6 2EH
020 7371 5400
Page 29bl

Story
020 7377 6377
Furniture, accessories.
*Pages 39r, 49, 65,
128bl, 135l*

Stutchbury & Pape
Architecture
4/364 Barrenjoey Road
Newport NSW 2106
Australia
+61 2 9979 5030
snpala@ozemail.
com.au
Page 132a

Bruno Tanquerel
Artist
2 Passage St Sébastien
75011 Paris, France
+33 1 43 57 03 93
Page 117

**Touch Interior
Design**
020 7498 6409
Page 37

**Urban Research
Laboratory**
Ground Floor, Lime
Wharf, Vyner Street
London E2 9DJ
020 8709 9060
www.urbanresearch
lab.com
Page 106

**Voon Wong &
Benson Saw**
27, 1 Stannary Street
London SE11 4AD
020 7587 0116
www.voon-
benson.co.uk
Page 68

José de Yturbe
De Yturbe Arquitectos
Patriotisimo 13 (4° piso)
Lomas de Barrilaco
Mexico 11010 DF
+525 540 368
deyturbe infosel.net.mx
Pages 27, 59

Consuelo Zoelly
5–7 rue Mont Louis
75011 Paris, France
+33 1 42 62 19 95
Pages 88–89

PICTURE CREDITS

Key: **a**=above, **b**=below, **l**=left, **r**=right, **c**=centre,
ph=photographer

1 ph David Montgomery; **2 ph** Andrew Wood/Alastair Hendy
and John Clinch's apartment in London designed by
Alastair Hendy; **2–3 ph** David Brittain; **3al ph** Ray Main/Lee
F. Mindel's apartment in New York designed by Shelton,
Mindel & Associates with Associate Architect Reed
Morrison, lighting designed by Johnson Schwinghammer;
3br ph James Morris/Skywood House near London designed
by Graham Phillips; **4 ph** David Montgomery; **5 ph** Polly
Wreford; **7 ph** David Brittain; **8 ph** Polly Wreford/Clare
Nash's house in London; **8–9 ph** Andrew Wood/Alastair
Hendy and John Clinch's apartment in London designed by
Alastair Hendy; **10–11 ph** Simon Upton; **12–13 ph** Simon
Upton/Barefoot Elegance; **14al ph** James Merrell; **14br ph**
Andrew Wood/a house in London designed by Guy
Stansfeld (020 7727 0133); **15 ph** Ray Main/Robert
Callender and Elizabeth Ogilvie's studio in Fife designed
by John C. Hope Architects; **16 ph** Tom Leighton/Roger
and Fay Oates' house in Herefordshire, The Long Barn,
Eastnor, Ledbury, Herefordshire HR8 1EL (01531
632718); **17 ph** Ray Main/Mark Jennings' apartment in
New York designed by Asfour Guzy; **18 ph** Simon Upton;
18–19 ph Henry Bourne; **20 ph** Polly Wreford/Lena
Proudlock's house in Gloucestershire; **21l&r ph** Polly
Wreford; **22 ph** Ray Main/light from Atrium; **23 ph** Andrew
Wood/Nicki de Metz's flat in London designed by de Metz
Architects; **24 ph** Ray Main/client's residence, East
Hampton,NY, designed by ZG Design; **25 ph** Ray Main/
Jonathan Leitersdorf's apartment in New York designed
by Jonathan Leitersdorf/Just Design Ltd; **26 ph** Tom
Leighton/Siobhan Squire and Gavin Lyndsey's loft in
London designed by Will White, 326 Portobello Road,
London W10 5RU (020 8964 8052); **27 ph** Simon Upton;
28 ph Alan Williams/Gail and Barry Stephen's house in
London; **29al ph** Ray Main/Lee F. Mindel's apartment in
New York designed by Shelton, Mindel & Associates with
Associate Architect Reed Morrison, lighting designed by
Johnson Schwinghammer; **29bl ph** Ray Main/Jonathan
Reed's apartment in London, lighting designed by Sally
Storey, Design Director of John Cullen Lighting; **29r ph**
Alan Williams/Andrew Wallace's house in London; **30 ph**
Simon Upton/Barefoot Elegance; **31 ph** Simon Upton;
32 ph Andrew Wood/Heidi Kingstone's apartment in London;
32–33 ph David Brittain; **33r ph** Simon Upton/Barefoot
Elegance; **34l ph** Catherine Gratwicke/Karen Harrison's
house in London, cushions from Mint; **34r ph** Catherine

Gratwicke/Intérieurs in New York; **35 ph** Polly Wreford/Adria
Ellis' apartment in New York, painting by Peter Zangrillo;
36 inset ph Henry Bourne; **36 background ph** James Merrell;
37 ph Alan Williams/Katie Bassford King's house in London
designed by Touch Interior Design; **38al ph** James Merrell;
38bl ph Andrew Wood; **38r ph** Simon Upton/Barefoot
Elegance; **39l ph** James Merrell; **39r ph** Polly Wreford/Ann
Shore's house in London; **40a ph** Polly Wreford/Adria Ellis'
apartment in New York; **41 ph** Simon Upton; **42a ph** David
Brittain; **42b ph** Catherine Gratwicke/Kimball Mayer and
Megan Hughes' apartment in New York, designed by L.A.
Morgan; **43 ph** Simon Upton/Barefoot Elegance; **44 ph**
David Brittain; **45l ph** James Merrell; **45ra ph** Chris
Everard; **45rb ph** David Brittain; **46–47 all ph** David
Brittain; **48 ph** James Merrell; **49 ph** Polly Wreford/Ann
Shore's house in London; **50l ph** Ray Main; **50r & 50–51 ph**
Simon Upton; **52 ph** Tom Leighton; **53a ph** Ray Main/Jamie
Falla's house in London designed by MooArc; **53b ph** Tom
Leighton/ceramic jars Carden Cunietti; **54a ph** Chris
Everard; **54b ph** Alan Williams/Ms Feldman's house in New
York by Patricia Seidman of Mullman Seidman Architects;
55 ph Alan Williams/Warner Johnson's apartment in New
York designed by Edward Cabot at Cabot Design Ltd;
56 & 57l&ar ph James Merrell, **57br ph** Andrew Wood/
Heidi Kingstone's apartment in London; **58l ph** Henry
Bourne/Linda Trahair's house in Bath; **58c&r ph** Andrew
Wood/Roger and Fay Oates' house in Herefordshire, The
Long Barn, Eastnor, Ledbury, Herefordshire HR8 1EL
(01531 632718); **59 ph** Simon Upton; **60 ph** Andrew
Wood/Alastair Hendy and John Clinch's apartment in
London designed by Alastair Hendy; **61 ph** Andrew
Wood/Han Feng's apartment in New York designed by
Han Feng; **62 & 63l ph** Andrew Wood/Bernie De Le Cuona's
house in Windsor; **63r ph** David Brittain; **64a ph** Andrew
Wood/Mary Shaw's Sequana apartment in Paris; **64b ph**
Tom Leighton/Farrow & Ball colours; **64 background ph**
Tom Leighton; **65 ph** Polly Wreford/Ann Shore's house in
London; **66 ph** Andrew Wood; **67l ph** Caroline Arber/Linda
Garman's home in London; **67r ph** Polly Wreford; **68 ph**
Alan Williams/the architect Voon Wong's own apartment in
London; **68–69 ph** Polly Wreford/Marie-Hélène de Taillac's
pied-à-terre in Paris; **70–71 ph** Ray Main/Marina and Peter
Hill's barn in West Sussex designed by Marina Hill, Peter
James Construction Management, Chichester, The West
Sussex Antique Timber Company, Wisborough Green, and
Joanna Jefferson Architects; **72–73 all ph** Tom Leighton;
74l&r ph James Merrell; **75 ph** Ray Main/Lee F. Mindel's
apartment in New York designed by Shelton, Mindel &

Associates with Associate Architect Reed Morrison, lighting designed by Johnson Schwinghammer; **76 ph** Tom Leighton/Siobhan Squire and Gavin Lyndsey's loft in London designed by Will White, 326 Portobello Road, London W10 5RU (020 8964 8052); **77l ph** Polly Wreford/Carol Reid's apartment in Paris; **77ar ph** Chris Everard/Justin de Syllas and Annette Main's house in London, light courtesy of Artemide; **77br ph** Polly Wreford; **78l&r ph** Andrew Wood/Guido Palau's house in North London designed by Azman Associates (formerly Azman Owens Architects); **79 ph** James Merrell/an apartment in London designed by Ash Sakula Architects; **80 ph** Simon Upton; **80–81 ph** Andrew Wood/an apartment in Knokke, Belgium designed by Claire Bataille and Paul ibens; **82 ph** Tom Leighton; **83al&br ph** Simon Upton; **83ar & 84al ph** Polly Wreford; **84br ph** David Montgomery; **85 ph** Caroline Arber; **86 ph** James Merrell; **86–87 ph** Simon Upton; **88al&bl ph** James Merrell; **88–89 ph** James Merrell/ Consuelo Zoelly's apartment in Paris; **89 ph** James Merrell/ an apartment in London designed by Ash Sakula Architects; **90 ph** James Merrell/Mike and Kris Taylor's loft in London designed by Circus Architects with Kayode Lipede; **91al&bl ph** James Merrell; **91r & 92al ph** David Loftus; **92bl ph** David Brittain; **92r ph** James Merrell; **93 ph** Andrew Wood/a house in London designed by Bowles & Linares; **94 ph** David Brittain; **95 ph** Ray Main/Seth Stein's house in London; **96a ph** David Loftus; **96b ph** David Brittain; **97 ph** Andrew Wood/Lims' house designed by Bedmar & Shi Designers in Singapore; **98–99 ph** Ray Main/a house in London designed by Mark Guard Architects; **100a&b ph** Tom Leighton/a loft in London designed by Robert Dye Associates; **100 background ph** Polly Wreford; **101 ph** James Merrell; **102–103 all ph** Simon Upton; **104l ph** Tom Leighton/Roger and Fay Oates' house in Herefordshire, The Long Barn, Eastnor, Ledbury, Herefordshire HR8 1EL (01531 632718); **104ar ph** Polly Wreford/Kimberly Watson's house in London; **104br ph** Polly Wreford/Ros Fairman's house in London; **105 ph** Polly Wreford/Carol Reid's apartment in Paris; **106 ph** Alan Williams/an apartment for Richard Oyarzarbal, by Urban Research Laboratory, London; **107a ph** Andrew Wood/Heidi Kingstone's apartment in London; **107bl ph** Ray Main/Kirk and Caroline Pickering's house in London, space creation by Square Foot Properties Ltd; **107br ph** Henry Bourne; **108l&r ph** Alan Williams/Alannah Weston's house in London designed by Stickland Coombe Architecture; **109l ph** Ray Main/a loft in London designed by Nico Rensch, light from SKK; **109r ph** James Merrell; **110–111 ph** Chris Everard/a house in Hampstead, London designed by Orefelt Associates; **112l ph** Andrew Wood/a house in London designed by Guy Stansfeld (020 7727 0133); **112r ph** Polly Wreford/Kathy Moskal's apartment in New York designed by Ken Foreman; **113 ph** Chris Everard/a house in Surrey refurbished by Damien D'Arcy Associates; **114 & 115l ph** Chris Everard/Sugarman–Behun house on Long Island; **115 ph** David Montgomery; **116l ph** Andrew Wood/a house at Jalan Berjaya, Singapore designed by Chan Soo Khian of SCDA Architects; **116r ph** Chris Everard; **117 ph** Chris Everard/a house in Paris designed by Bruno Tanquerel; **118–119 ph** Andrew Wood/a house near Antwerp designed by Claire Bataille and Paul ibens; **119a ph** Chris Everard/Simon Brignall and Christina Rosetti's loft in London designed by David Mikhail; **119b ph** Andrew Wood/a house near Antwerp designed by Claire Bataille and Paul ibens; **120 ph** Alan Williams/ Alannah Weston's house in London designed by Stickland Coombe Architecture; **121al&ar ph** Chris Everard/Hilton McConnico's (interior house designer) house near Paris; **121b ph** Henry Bourne/Dan and Claire Thorne's townhouse in Dorset designed by Sarah Featherstone; **122–123 ph** Polly Wreford; **124l ph** Polly Wreford/Marie-Hélène de Taillac's pied-à-terre in Paris; **124r ph** Ray Main/light: Tizio by Richard Sapper, manufacturer: Artemide; **125l&r ph** Andrew Wood/Babylon Design Ltd, studio in London; **126 ph** Polly Wreford/an apartment in New York designed by Belmont Freeman Architects; **127al ph** Ray Main/Thierry Watorek's house near Paris; **127bl ph** Ray Main/light by Tsé Tsé Associées, Catherine Levy and Sigolene Prebois; **127r ph** Ray Main/light: Babylon Design Ltd; **128a ph** Henry Bourne; **128bl ph** Polly Wreford/Ann Shore's house in London; **129 ph** Andrew Wood; **130–131 ph** James Morris/Skywood House near London designed by Graham Phillips; **132a ph** Jan Baldwin/Robert and Gabrielle Reeves' house in Clareville designed by Stutchbury & Pape Architects; **132b ph** Andrew Wood/Johanne Riss' house in Brussels; **133 ph** Ray Main/client's residence, East Hampton, NY, designed by ZG Design; **134 ph** Jan Baldwin/Terry and Heather Dorrough's house on Dangar Island, NSW, designed by Terry Dorrough, architect; **135l ph** Polly Wreford/Ann Shore's house in London; **135r ph** James Merrell/a house in Pennsylvania designed by Laura Bohn and built by Richard Fiore/BFI Construction; **136 ph** Andrew Wood/Lims' house designed by Bedmar & Shi Designers in Singapore; **137 ph** Jan Baldwin/Les Reedman's house on Dangar Island, NSW.

index